Hypnosis

Medical,

Scientific,

or

Occultic?

Martin and Deidre Bobgan
EastGate Publishers

Hypnosis: Medical, Scientific, or Occultic?

Copyright © 2001 Martin and Deidre Bobgan
Published by EastGate Publishers
4137 Primavera Road
Santa Barbara, California 93110

Library of Congress Catalog Card Number 2001089389
ISBN 0-941717-18-6

Printed in the United States of America

Table of Contents

1

Hypnotic Origins

Hypnosis has been used as a method of mental, emotional, behavioral, and physical healing for hundreds and even thousands of years.[1] Witchdoctors, Sufi practitioners, shamans, Hindus, Buddhists, and yogis have practiced hypnosis, and now medical doctors, dentists, psychotherapists, and others have joined them. From witchdoctors to medical doctors and from past to present, the rituals and results have been reproduced, revised, and repeated.

The hypnotic trance begins by focusing a person's attention and produces many results. According to its advocates, the practice of hypnotism may alter behavior in such a way as to change habits; stimulate the mind to recall forgotten events and information; enable a person to overcome shyness, fears, and depression; cure maladies such as asthma and hayfever; improve a person's sex life; and remove pain.[2]

Fantastic claims and the increasing popularity of hypnosis in the secular world have influenced many in the church to turn to hypnotism for help. Various Christian medical doctors, dentists, psychiatrists, psychologists and counselors are using hypnosis in their practices and recommending its use for Christians.

Christians who support the use of hypnosis do so for some of the same reasons medical doctors and psychotherapists recommend it. These Christians believe that hypnosis is scientific rather than occultic when it is practiced by a qualified professional. They distinguish between those who practice it for helpful purposes and those who use it with evil intent. They believe it is a safe and useful tool in the hands of professionally trained, benevolent individuals, even though hypnotism can be dangerous in the hands of malevolent individuals or novices. Furthermore, they believe that it is safe because they see hypnosis as an extension of natural, everyday experiences. Finally, they contend that a person's will is not violated during the hypnotic trance.

Many in the church believe that hypnosis can be either scientific or satanic, depending upon the practitioner and the purpose for which it is used. Cult-critic Walter Martin endorsed the use of hypnosis by medical doctors for some of the reasons just mentioned.[3] Josh McDowell and Don Stewart, authors of *Understanding the Occult,* say, "If a person allows himself to be hypnotized, it should be only under the most controlled situation by a qualified and experienced physician."[4]

We have letters from Christian psychologists, medical doctors, and psychiatrists who not only use hypnosis, but are critical of those who recommend against it. One medical doctor, who refers to himself as a "born again Christian" and "a board certified psychiatrist," inferred that we had twisted things "to fit

[our]concepts" and wanted a more "balanced view."[5] H. Newton Maloney, a professor in the Graduate School of Theology at Fuller Seminary, wrote a position paper defending the use of hypnosis.[6] Also, *The Christian Medical Society Journal* has run articles supportive of hypnosis, which were written by Christian medical doctors.[7]

Hypnosis was once taboo, but now its use is encouraged under certain circumstances and many Christians have become confused over the issue. However, before we allow hypnotism to become the new panacea for the parishioner, we need to examine its claims, methods and long-term results.

Origins of Modern Hypnosis

Modern hypnosis evolved from an eighteenth-century phenomenon known as mesmerism. The word *hypnosis* was coined in the 1840s by a Scottish physician by the name of James Braid, who used the Greek word *hypnos*, because he thought mesmerism resembled sleep.[8]

Austrian physician Friedrich (Franz) Anton Mesmer believed he had discovered the great universal cure of both physical and emotional problems. In 1779 he announced, "There is only one illness and one healing."[9] Mesmer presented the idea that an invisible fluid was distributed throughout the body. He called the fluid "animal magnetism" and believed it influenced illness or health in both the mental-emotional and the physical aspects of life. He considered this fluid to be an energy existing throughout nature. He taught that proper health and mental well-being came from the proper distribution and balance of animal magnetism throughout the body.

Mesmer's ideas may sound rather foolish from a scientific point of view. However, they were well received. Furthermore, as they were modified they formed much of the basis for present-day psychotherapy. The most important modification of mesmerism was getting rid of the magnets. Through a series of progressions, the animal magnetism theory moved from the place of the physical effect of magnets to the psychological affects of mind over matter. Thus the awkward passing of magnets across the body of a person sitting in a tub of water was eliminated.

The History of Psychotherapy reveals the earlier occult origins of Mesmer's work. It says:

> He regarded all illnesses as the manifestations of disturbances in a mysterious ethereal fluid which linked together animate and inanimate things alike, and which made man equally subject to the influences of the stars and to those influences emanating from Dr. Mesmer himself. This is what Mesmer described as animal, in contrast to "ordinary," magnetism. His theories thus reach back to ancient astrological and magical concepts.[10]

Erika Fromm and Ronald Shor, editors of a text on hypnosis, say:

> Mesmer's therapy and theory were minor variants of the teachings of many other faith healers throughout history. His therapy was a combination of the ancient procedure of laying on of hands with a disguised version of medieval demonic exorcism. His theory was a combination of ancient

astrological concepts, medieval mysticism, and seventeenth-century vitalism.[11]

Although hypnosis had been used for centuries in various occult activities, including medium trances, Mesmer and his followers brought it into the respectable realm of Western medicine. And, with the shift in emphasis from the physical manipulation of magnets to so-called psychological powers hidden in the depths of the mind, mesmerism moved from the physical to the psychological and spiritual.

Mesmerism became psychological rather than physical with patients moving into trance-like states. Furthermore, some of the subjects of mesmerism moved into deeper states of consciousness and spontaneously engaged in telepathy, precognition, and clairvoyance.[12] Gradually mesmerism evolved into an entire view of life. Mesmerism presented a new way of healing people through conversation with an instant rapport between a practitioner and his subject. Those involved in medicine used mesmerism in their investigation of supposed unseen reservoirs of potential for healing within the mind.

Mesmerism incited much interest in America when a Frenchman by the name of Charles Poyen lectured and conducted exhibitions during the 1830s. Audiences were impressed with the feats of mesmerism because hypnotized subjects would spontaneously exercise clairvoyance and mental telepathy. While under the spell, subjects could also experience and report deeper levels of consciousness in which they said they could feel utter unity with the universe beyond the confines of space and time. Furthermore, they would give apparent supernatural information and diagnose diseases telepathically. This led people to believe that great untapped powers of the mind were available to them.[13]

The thrust of mesmerism also changed directions in America.[14] In his book *Mesmerism and the American Cure of Souls,* Robert Fuller describes how it promised great psychological and spiritual advantages. Its promises for self improvement, spiritual experience, and personal fulfillment were especially welcomed by unchurched individuals. Fuller says that mesmerism offered "an entirely new and eminently attractive arena for self-discovery—their own psychological depths." He says that "its theories and methods promised to restore individuals, even unchurched ones, into harmony with the cosmic scheme."[15] Fuller's description of mesmerism in America is an accurate portrayal of twentieth-century psychotherapy as well as of so-called mind-science religions.

Fuller reveals that "the American mesmerists described at least six distinct levels of psychological reality."[16] The first five levels include the following characteristics: "Catalepsy. Rigidity of the muscles"; "the mind is open to impressions coming directly from the environment without reliance upon the five physical senses"; "telepathy, clairvoyance, and other feats of extra sensory perception."[17] The sixth or deepest level is described as follows:

> At this deepest level of consciousness, subjects feel themselves to be united with the creative principle of the universe (animal magnetism). There is a mystical sense of intimate rapport with the cosmos. Subjects feel that they are in possession of knowledge which transcends that of physical,

space-time reality. Those who enter this state are able to use it for diagnosing the nature and causes of physical illness. They are also able to exert control over these magnetic healing energies so as to cure persons even at a considerable physical distance. Telepathy, cosmic consciousness, and mystical wisdom all belong to this deepest level of consciousness discovered in the mesmerists' experiments.[18]

Because of these experiences, Fuller says:

It was inevitable that the mesmerists' psychological continuum would be thought also to define a metaphysical hierarchy. That is, the "deeper" levels of consciousness opened the individual to qualitatively "higher" places of mental existence. The mesmerists confidently proclaimed that the key to achieving personal harmony with these deeper levels of ultimate reality lies quite literally within ourselves.[19]

After discussing the spiritual dimensions of Mesmerism, Fuller says:

The mind curists' pantheistic ontology made conventional theology more or less irrelevant. The only barrier separating individuals from spiritual abundance was understood to be a psychological one. In this way, mesmerist theories had done away with the necessity of repentance or contrition as a means of reconciling oneself with God's will. Obedience to the laws of the mind, not to scriptural commandments, is what enables God's presence

to manifest itself in our lives. The path of spiritual progress was one of systematic self-adjust-
ment.[20]

Mesmerism and hypnosis produce the same results.
Hypnosis is merely contemporary mesmerism. The
users of mesmerism did not suspect the occult
connections of hypnosis. Both the practitioners and
subjects believed that hypnosis revealed untapped
reservoirs of human possibility and powers. They
believed that these powers could be used to understand
the self, to attain perfect health, to develop supernatural gifts, and to reach spiritual heights. Thus, the goal
and impetus for discovering and developing human
potential grew out of mesmerism and stimulated the
growth and expansion of psychotherapy, positive thinking, the human potential movement, and the mind-
science religions, as well as the growth and expansion
of hypnosis itself.

The theories and practices of mesmerism greatly
influenced the up-and-coming field of psychiatry with
such early men as Jean Martin Charcot, Pierre Janet,
and Sigmund Freud. These men used information
gleaned from patients in the hypnotic state.[21] Hypnosis led to the belief that the there is an unconscious
part of the mind that is filled with powerful material
which motivates actions, a hidden powerful self that
directs and controls the feelings, thoughts and actions
of individuals. Mesmer's influence on Freud led him to
develop an entire psychodynamic theory. Freud
believed that the unconscious portion of the mind,
rather than the conscious, influences all of a person's
thoughts and actions. He taught that the unconscious
not only influences, but determines what individuals

do and think. Freud considered this mental set to be established within the unconscious during the first five years of life. According to his theory, traumas of the past, locked into one's unconscious, compel thoughts and control behavior. He theorized that if one could tap into this unconscious, people could be healed of neuroses and psychoses. Professor of psychiatry Thomas Szasz describes Mesmer's influence this way:

> Insofar as psychotherapy as a modern "medical technique" can be said to have a discoverer, Mesmer was that person, Mesmer stands in the same sort of relation to Freud and Jung as Columbus stands in relation to Thomas Jefferson and John Adams. Columbus stumbled onto a continent that the founding fathers subsequently transformed into the political entity known as the United States of America. Mesmer stumbled onto the literalized use of the leading scientific metaphor of his age for explaining and exorcising all manner of human problems and passions, a rhetorical device that the founders of modern depth psychology subsequently transformed into the pseudomedical entity known as psychotherapy.[22]

The followers of Mesmer promoted the ideas of hypnotic suggestion, healing through talking, and mind-over-matter. Thus, the three main thrusts of Mesmer's influence were hypnosis, psychotherapy, and positive thinking.

Mesmer's far reaching influence gave an early impetus to scientific-sounding religious alternatives to Christianity. He also started the trend of medicalizing religion into treatment and therapy. Nevertheless, he only gave the world false religion and false hope.

In medicalizing hypnosis, Mesmer and his follow-ers have made hypnosis respectable to the general public and caused Christians to be more vulnerable to its claims and promises. Therefore, Christians need to be informed and forearmed with answers to the following questions: What exactly is hypnosis? Is it a natural experience? How are people induced? Are they deceived? Can the will be violated? What happens during hypnosis? Is hypnosis medical, scientific, or occultic? What does the Bible say about hypnosis?

2

What Is Hypnosis?

Through hypnosis, practitioners and patients hope to uncover hidden realms within themselves. Through these means they attempt to discover memories, emotions, desires, doubts, fears, insecurities, powers, and even secret knowledge buried deep within what they believe is a powerful unconscious, determining behavior quite apart from and even against conscious choice. The allure is to tap into what they believe to be a huge reservoir for healing and for power. Thus hypnosis is touted to activate hidden resources for extraordinary powers and for healing. Consider such promises made by enterprising hypnotists: self-mastery, personal well-being, emotional healing and health, the ability to overcome addictions, to create wealth, and to influence others at the unconscious or subconscious level.

In answering the question, "What is Hypnosis?" *The Harvard Mental Health Letter* says:

Although it has become familiar through more than two hundred years of use as entertainment,

15

self-help, and therapy, the hypnotic trance remains a remarkably elusive, even mysterious psychological state. Most of us may think we know what hypnosis is, but few could say if asked. Although even experts do not fully agree on how to define it, they usually emphasize three related features: absorption or selective attention, suggestibility, and dissociation.[1]

Confusion reigns in the field of hypnosis because there is so much disagreement regarding what it is. William Kroger and William Fezler, in their book *Hypnosis and Behavior Modification*, say, "There are as many definitions of hypnosis as there are definers."[2] Some people are very precise as to what it is and what it isn't. However, Kroger's definition is so expanded that he titled a presentation "No Matter How You Slice It, It's Hypnosis." His definition of hypnosis includes alpha waves, biofeedback, suggestology, focusing, prayer, communion, relaxation, Lamaze childbirthing, and all forms of psychotherapy. Of course, if Kroger is correct and all life activities involve hypnosis, then it would be difficult to criticize it without being critical of all sorts of life activities.[3] If everything were hypnosis, one would almost have to withdraw from life to avoid it.

In his book *They Call It Hypnosis*, Robert Baker states the issue concisely and precisely:

There is no single topic in the history of psychology more controversial than hypnosis. From its beginning in the middle of the eighteenth century with Franz Anton Mesmer to the present, the phenomenon has been mired in controversy.[4]

The very definition of hypnosis ranges from "It does not exist" to "Everything is hypnosis." Even though Baker has written two books on hypnosis, he does not believe it even exists. He contends:

> Strictly speaking, every time the word "hypnosis" is used it could be placed in quotation marks. This is because there is no such thing as hypnosis . . . the phenomenon called "hypnosis" does not exist, has never existed in the past, and will not exist in the future.[5]

Some theories explain hypnosis as being like the psychoanalytic phenomenon of transference. One text defines transference as "Projection of feelings, thoughts, and wishes onto the therapist, who has come to represent an object from the patient's past."[6] It further states:

> Hypnotized patients are in a state of atypical dependence on the therapist, and so a strong transference may develop characterized by a positive attachment that must be respected and interpreted.[7]

In fact Baker insists that the hypnotist "is important only as a transference figure." The hypnotist and client each assume a role in a relationship that gives the hypnotist all power and authority over the client. Baker says that the hypnotist takes advantage of his position as an authority figure and allows the client to fantasize that he has power over the hypnotized person. The client thus believes that the hypnotist is the one who is responsible for whatever happens during the trance.[8]

Through this relationship with the physician or hypnotist "patients can and will produce symptoms to please their physicians."[9] According to this theory, hypnotized people play a role to please the hypnotist. This very popular view opposes the view that hypnotized people enter a distinct psychological state.

One group of researchers put this notion to the test. At the conclusion of their research they say: "These findings support the claim that hypnosis is a psychological state with distinct neural correlates and is not just the result of adopting a role."[10] The authors say, "hypnosis is not simply role enactment," but that "changes in brain function" occur.[11] Thus, **hypnotized individuals do enter a distinct psychological state.**

Dr. David Spiegel, Professor of Psychiatry and Behavioral Sciences at Stanford University says:

> Some have argued that hypnosis involves no unusual state of consciousness, that it is merely a response to social cues. Most investigators disagree. . . . On EEG examinations, easily hypnotized people have more electrical activity of the type known as theta waves in the left frontal region of the cerebral cortex. Studies measuring the brain's electrical responses to stimuli show specific hypnotic effects on perception. . . . In two recent studies, measurements of blood flow and metabolic activity by positron emission tomography (PET) have shown that hypnosis activates a part of the brain involved in focusing attention, the anterior cingulate gyrus. There is also evidence that it enhances the activity of dopamine, a neurotransmitter involved in planning, memory, and

movement. Thus hypnosis is a neurophysiological reality as well as a psychological and social one.[12]

Research has indicated a degree of dissociation during hypnosis, in that, as the hypnotized person focuses on one object or thought, competing thoughts or sensations are ignored. He does not consider whether his actions make sense and fails to consider consequences.[13]

Many researchers thus conclude that hypnosis is an altered state of consciousness, which may also be considered a trance state. Erika Fromm, who is a psychologist at the University of Chicago and considered an expert on the clinical uses of hypnosis says:

> Most experts agree that hypnosis is an altered state of consciousness involving highly focused attention and heightened absorption and imagery, increased susceptibility to suggestion, and closer contact with the unconscious.[14]

Hypnosis, Trance, and Altered States of Consciousness

The following are definitions of hypnosis or the trance state from several different sources:

> Hypnosis is an altered condition or state of consciousness characterized by a markedly increased receptivity to suggestion, the capacity for modification of perception and memory, and the potential for systematic control of a variety of usually involuntary physiological functions (such as glandular activity, vasomotor activity, etc.). Further, the experience of hypnosis creates an unusual

relationship between the person offering the suggestions and the person receiving them.[15]

Persons under hypnosis are said to be in a trance state, which may be light, medium, or heavy (deep). In a light trance there are changes in motor activity such that the person's muscles can feel relaxed, the hands can levitate, and paresthesia [e.g., prickling skin sensation] can be induced. A medium trance is characterized by diminished pain sensation and partial or complete amnesia. A deep trance is associated with induced visual or auditory experiences and deep anesthesia. Time distortion occurs at all trance levels but is most profound in the deep trance.[16]

Hypnotic "trance" is not either/or but lies on a continuum ranging from hypnoidal relaxation to "deep" states of involvement. Although many patients make favorable responses to suggestions when lightly hypnotized, for best results it is usually considered wise to induce as deep a state as possible before beginning treatment. The techniques of hypnotic induction are many, but most include suggestions of relaxation, monotonous stimulation, involvement in fantasy, activation of unconscious motives, and initiation of regressive behavior.[17]

The following are the twelve most common phenomenological characteristics of the trance experience:

1. Experiential absorption of attention.
2. Effortless expression.

3. Experiential, non-conceptual involvement.
4. Willingness to experiment.
5. Flexibility in time/space relations.
6. Alteration of sensory experience.
7. Fluctuation in involvement.
8. Motoric/verbal inhibition.
9. Trance Logic.
10. Metaphorical processing.
11. Time distortion.
12. Amnesia.[18]

Two of the many interesting facts we discovered while researching hypnosis are the lack of long-term research on its aftereffects and the similarity to occult states of consciousness that have ancient origins. The scarcity of long-term studies raises questions about effects of hypnosis on people's spiritual lives. Also, we looked into shamans and shamanism. A shaman is also known as a witch, witchdoctor, medicine man, sorcerer, wizard, magic man, magician, and seer.[19]

In *The Way of the Shaman*, Michael Harner says:

A shaman is a man or woman who enters an altered state of consciousness—at will—to contact and utilize an ordinarily hidden reality in order to acquire knowledge, power, and to help other persons. A shaman has at least one, and usually more, 'spirits' in his personal service.[20]

This altered state of consciousness is called a shamanic state of consciousness (SSC). We found no difference between the SSC and the altered state of consciousness known as hypnosis. While each might be used for different purposes, both are equivalent trance states.

We again raise the question of its aftereffects on people's spiritual lives.

At the same time we were researching and writing on hypnosis, we were also looking into the area of near death experiences (NDE). Dr. Kenneth Ring, a professor of psychology, is one of the best-known researchers in the field of NDE. Ring's book *Heading Toward Omega: In Search of the Meaning of the Near-Death Experience* is considered a classic.[21] In reviewing Kenneth Ring's book on near-death experiences, Stanislov Grof says:

> Ring presents convincing evidence indicating that the NDE has been established as a certifiable phenomenon, which occurs in about 35-40% of the people who come close to death. He suggests that the core of the NDE is essentially deep spiritual experience characterized by visions of light of overwhelming brilliance and with certain personal characteristics, feelings of all-embracing pure love, sense of forgiveness and total acceptance, telepathic exchange with the being of light, access to knowledge of universal nature, and understanding of one's life and true values.
>
> The core NDE is a powerful catalyst of spiritual awakening and consciousness evolution. Its long-term aftereffects include increase in self-esteem and self-confidence, appreciation of life and nature, concern and love for fellow humans, decrease of interest in personal status and material possessions, **more open attitude toward reincarnation, and development of universal spirituality that transcends the divisive interests of religious sectarianism and resembles the**

best of the mystical traditions or great Oriental philosophies. These changes are remarkably similar to those described by Maslow following spontaneous peak experiences and also transcendental experience in psychedelic sessions.

Of special interest is Ring's discussion of the parallels between NDE and the phenomena associated with Kundalini awakening, as described in traditional Indian scriptures.[22] (Bold added.)

We wondered if in the future, after someone has been hypnotized and particularly been brought into a deep trance, the person would share characteristics similar to the above description of those having had an NDE. Ring, speaking on the subject of NDEs and other transcendental experiences proposes:

Might it be then that what we are witnessing, taking into account the growth of these particular kinds of transcendental experiences, are the beginning stages of the shamanizing of humanity and thereby of humanity's finding its way back to its true home in the realm of the imagination where we will live in mythic time and no longer just in historical time. In other words, in this period of apparently rapidly accelerating evolutionary pressure, is it the case that these two worlds might in some way be drawing closer to one another so that, like the traditional shaman, we, too, will find it easy to cross the bridge between the worlds and live comfortably and at ease in both of them?[23]

The *Concise Textbook* describes aspects of the trance state, which may occur in other contexts besides hypnosis:

> Possession and trance states are curious and imperfectly understood forms of dissociation. A common example of a trance state is the medium who presides over a spiritual séance. Typically, mediums enter a dissociative state, during which a person from the so-called spirit world takes over much of the mediums' conscious awareness and influences their thoughts and speech.
>
> Automatic writing and crystal-gazing are less common manifestations of possession or trance states. In automatic writing the dissociation affects only the arm and the hand that write the message, which often discloses mental contents of which the writer was unaware. Crystal-gazing results in a trance state in which visual hallucinations are prominent.[24]

Hypnosis is a discreet state of consciousness in which the same things occur as in various descriptions of trance states. Moreover, those who are particularly susceptible to hypnosis are also those who readily respond to suggestion and easily engage in visualization, fantasy, and imagination. The *Concise Encyclopedia of Psychology* (*Concise Encyclopedia*) lists a number of characteristics of the good hypnotic subjects and gives a profile of how many investigators view them:

> The typical hypnotizable person has the capacity to become totally absorbed in ongoing experiences (e.g., becoming lost in fantasy or empathetically

identifying with the emotions of a character in a play or movie). He or she reports imaginary playmates as a youngster.[25]

Imagery, Fantasy, Visualization

Ernest Hilgard, who has been studying hypnosis for over twenty-five years, has discovered that not everyone is prone to being hypnotized. He found that "those who can immerse themselves in fantasy and imagination" are the most ideal hypnotic subjects.[26] *Psychology Today,* reporting on a study of hypnosis, states that such an individual (referred to as a somnambule) "has a highly developed capacity for extreme fantasy and is likely to indulge it frequently without benefit of hypnosis." This study revealed that somnambules had the "ability to hallucinate at will" and "had powerful sexual fantasies." However, most alarming was the fact that *all* the somnambules in the study "believed that they had had psychic experiences, such as encounters with ghosts."[27]

"The active ingredient in hypnosis is imagery," declares Daniel, Kohen, M.D., Associate Director of Behavior Pediatrics at the Minneapolis Children's Medical Center.[28] Medical doctor Jeanne Achterberg says, "I don't know any real difference between hypnosis and imagery."[29]

William Kroger says, "The images you use are the most potent form of therapy." He suggests that bad images make you sick and good images make you well. Kroger tells how he increases the power of the image. He says:

> We now give an image in five senses, because an image in five senses now makes the image more

potent. The more vivid the image, the more readily conditioning occurs.[30]

Josephine Hilgard, a well-known researcher in the field of hypnosis, as well as many other experts, believes "that hypnotizability is significantly related to the ability to fantasize."[31] Robert Baker contends that "the greater or better the individual's powers of imagination or fantasy, the easier it is for the individual to become hypnotized and to demonstrate all of the behavior others normally associate with or attach to the phenomenon of hypnosis."[32]

Those people who engage in fantasy and vivid visualization easily move into the hypnotic trance, whereas those who are not fantasy prone are less easily led into hypnosis. Most fantasy-prone individuals created fantasy worlds for themselves when they were children and continue to spend time fantasizing even as adults. However, they tend to keep these experiences to themselves. Many had make-believe friends when they were children and believed in fairies. Fantasy-prone individuals also claim supernatural powers, such as psychic, telepathic, and healing powers. They also report having vivid dreams. Baker says:

> The fantasy-prone individuals show up as mediums, psychics, and religious visionaries. They are also the ones who have many realistic "out-of-the-body" experiences and the prototypic "near-death" experience. However, the overwhelming majority of fantasy-pone personalities fall within the broad range of normally functioning persons, and it is totally inappropriate to label them psychiatric cases.[33]

The words *imagery* and *fantasy* appear often in reference to hypnosis. By their very nature, imagery and fantasy involve visualization. However, before warning about the practice of visualization and imagination involved in hypnosis, we must say that **there are ordinary, legitimate uses of the imagination**. For instance one may mentally see what is happening while reading a story or listening to a friend describe something. Imagination and visualization are normal activities for creating works of art and for developing architectural designs and even scientific theories.

However, visualization by suggestion through hypnosis may be so focused as to move the person into an altered state of consciousness with the visualization becoming more powerful than reality. Other dangerous uses of visualization in or out of a trance would be attempting to manipulate reality through focused mental power or conjuring up a spirit guide. Some people are led to imagine a quiet, beautiful place and once they are mentally there, the suggestion is made to wait for a special being (person or animal) who will guide them and reveal information important for their lives. That is a form of shamanism.

Dave Hunt warns about visualization in his book *Occult Invasion*:

> Occultism has always involved three techniques for changing and creating reality: thinking, speaking, and visualizing. . . .
>
> The third technique [visualizing] is the most powerful. It is the fastest way to enter the world of the occult and to pick up a spirit guide. Shamans have used it for thousands of years. It was taught to Carl Jung by spirit beings, and through

him influenced humanistic and transpersonal psychology. It was taught to Napoleon Hill by the spirits that began to guide him. Agnes Sanford . . . was the first to bring it into the church. Norman Vincent Peale was not far behind her, and his influence was much greater. . . .

Visualization has become an important tool among evangelicals as well—which doesn't purge it of its occult power. Yonggi Cho has made it the center of his teaching. In fact, he declares that no one can have faith unless he visualizes that for which he is praying. Yet the Bible states that faith is "the evidence of things not seen" (Hebrews 11:1). Thus visualization, the attempt to "see" the answer to one's prayer, would work *against* faith rather than help it! Yet Norman Vincent Peale declared, "If a person consciously visualizes being with Jesus that is the best guarantee I know for keeping the faith." [34]

Alan Morrison's book titled *The Serpent and the Cross: Religious Corruption in an Evil Age* includes a chapter titled "Sorcerous Apprentices: The Mind-Sciences in the Church Today," which should be read by all who are interested in hypnosis. A subsection in that chapter is titled "In Your Mind's Eye: The Occult Art of Visualization" and is a must-read for those who want to learn about the roots and promoters of visualization in the church. The following quotations are from that section:

Fundamental to our study is the fact that the development of the imagination through "visualization" exercises is one of the most ancient and widely used occult techniques for expanding the mind and opening up the psyche to new (and forbidden) areas of consciousness.[35]

The practice of visualization can be used in a variety of ways, but they all fall into three main types. **Firstly**, they can be used to provide a doorway into what psychologists call a "non-ordinary state of consciousness." **Secondly**, they can be used as a means towards something called "Inner Healing" or "Healing of the Memories." **Thirdly**, they can provide an instrument for the manipulation and recreation of matter and consciousness.[36]

Most of the people being seduced into the practice of visualization—especially those within the Church—have not the faintest conception of the occultic aim which lies at its root. In spite of the attractions and harmless benefits put forward by its advocates, visualization is a primary gateway for demonic infiltration into human consciousness—a deception currently being worked on a truly grand scale.[37]

Whatever hypnosis is, it does involve heightened suggestion, a discreet state of consciousness, trance phenomena, and aspects of dissociation, imagery, and visualization. Whatever hypnosis is, it can be a doorway into the occult.

3

Is Hypnosis a Natural Experience?

Those who promote hypnosis often say that hypnosis is a natural part of our everyday life. One example is Paul F. Barkman, clinical psychologist and Dean of Cedar Hill Institute for Graduate Studies, who says:

> Hypnotic trance occurs regularly in all Christian congregations. Those who most condemn it as diabolical are the very ones who tend to induce hypnotic trance most often—unaware that they are doing so.[1]

If by *natural* one means normal in the sense of sleep, then we reject this because sleep is a necessary part of life. Hypnosis is *not*. If by *natural* one means good, then we reject this too, because many natural emotions of humans, such as pride, anger, and jealousy, can be evil.

Professor Ernest Hilgard contends that "hypnosis is not something supernatural or frightening. It is perfectly normal and natural and follows from the conditions of attention and suggestion."[2] Hypnotist David Gordon thinks that a good salesman is a good hypnotist, a good movie involves hypnosis, and talking someone into doing something is a form of hypnosis. In fact, Gordon believes that "most of what people do is hypnosis."[3]

The purpose of those who promote hypnotism is to convince us that it is a part of our everyday life so that we will no longer be suspicious of it. Defining *hypnosis* as part of normal everyday living and a ubiquitous activity is a semantic twist to entice people into a trance. The logic presented is that "attention and suggestion" are a part of everyday life. Therefore, since hypnosis involves attention and suggestion it must be acceptable. With the same kind of logic, one could promote brainwashing. One person influencing another is part of everyday life. Brainwashing is merely one person influencing another. Through a process of *reductio ad absurdum* we are led to the idea that brainwashing is acceptable.

The similarities of hypnosis and natural states are superficial; but the deeper differences are enormous! Attention and suggestion are not hypnotism, and persuasion is not brainwashing. Attention and suggestion may be a part of hypnotism, and persuasion may be a part of brainwashing, but the whole is not equal to one part. Even psychic experiences and Eastern meditative techniques have some natural components.

If one can be convinced that hypnosis is a large part of his everyday thought life, then he will no longer be wary of it. One example used to support such a contention is that of a person who is watching the white stripe while driving on the freeway and misses his turn-off. This, we are told, is self-induced hypnosis. Does this mean that whenever one is focused on one thing and ignores another he has hypnotized himself? Some believe that any period of concentration is a form of hypnosis. They would say that if one travels from home to office and does not remember driving along the way, he is in a state of self-induced hypnosis. They would further suggest that if a person concentrates on relaxing in a fearful situation, such as during exams or interviews, he is employing the fundamentals of self-induced hypnosis.

Defining such events as self-hypnosis to give the entire field of hypnotism credibility is pure nonsense. The human choice to concentrate on relaxing instead of being fearful is no more hypnosis than choosing a football game over a movie or concentrating on one idea over another. If we stretch this ridiculous idea to its conclusion, we will end up labeling Christian conversion as a state of self-induced hypnosis. Not only would conversion be considered hypnosis, but so would repentance, communion, prayer, worship, and other elements of Christianity. And, this is exactly what has happened. Kroger and Fezler say, "A prime example of autohypnosis is prayer and meditation."[4] Kroger elsewhere says:

> Prayer, particularly in the Jewish and the Christian religions, has many similarities to hypnotic induction . . . the contemplation, the meditation, and the self-absorption characteristic of prayer are almost identical with autohypnosis.

Kroger contends that "The Old Testament prophets probably utilized both autohypnotic and mass-hypnotic techniques" and that "hypnosis in one form or another is practiced in nearly all religions." With respect to faith healing, Kroger adds:

> If one observes pilgrims expecting to be healed at a shrine, one is immediately impressed by the fact that the majority of these individuals, as they walk toward the shrine, are actually in a hypnotic state.

Kroger finally declares:

> The more one studies the various religions, from the most "primitive" to the most "civilized," the more one realizes that there is an astonishing relationship, involving suggestion and/or hypnosis as well as conditioning, between religious phenomena and hypnosis.[5]

Margaretta Bowers says:

> The religionist can no longer hide his head in the sand and claim ignorance of the science and art of the hypnotic discipline. . . . Whether he approves or disapproves, every effective religionist, in the usages of ritual, preaching, and worship, unavoidably makes use of hypnotic techniques.[6]

Richard Morton, an ordained minister with a Ph.D. in counseling psychology, has written a book titled *Hypnosis and Pastoral Counseling.* From his training and practice as a hypnotherapist and psychologist, Morton concludes that hypnosis is a normal human capacity and that to "attribute to that phenomenon per se a demonic or occultic status is to make God the author of evil." The purpose of his book is to encourage the religious community "to accept hypnosis with the honored status it so rightly deserves."[7] Morton describes the use of hypnotic techniques in the typical worship service. He says that "the experience of worship is predicated upon one's capacity for being susceptible to the hypnotic techniques utilized in worship."[8] Morton later says that "hypnosis, like religion, is natural, powerful and universal."[9]

To show how much one can pervert the truth, Morton, in a section titled "Hypnosis and Religion as Natural Phenomena," says:

> One of the earliest, if not the earliest, possible descriptions of hypnosis, is recorded in the book of Genesis in the Old Testament. Here, God is said to have "caused a deep sleep" to fall upon man in order to make for him a mate.[10]

In addition, Morton claims that the woman who came to Jesus with the issue of blood (Luke 8:43-48) was healed through hypnotism.[11] Morton believes that many of the healings of Jesus were performed through "natural" hypnotic means. And so, miracles are supposedly accomplished through hypnosis.

By reasoning that hypnosis is concentration and suggestion and that concentration and suggestion are hypnosis, one could be led to the conclusion that to resist hypnosis is to be opposed to communion, confession, conversion, and prayer. Carried to its extreme, in order to avoid hypnosis, one must give up his faith and stop thinking. If one applied this kind of reasoning to medicine, one might begin by noticing that medical doctors speak to their patients. Now one could conclude

that since medicine involves conversation, everyone
who converses is practicing medicine.

Although there are natural activities such as
concentration and suggestion in hypnosis, hypnotism
is not just a normal, everyday activity. Although there
may be similarities between prayer and hypnosis, there
is a great difference between yielding oneself to God
in prayer and yielding oneself to a hypnotist during
hypnosis. There is a big difference between believing
God and exercising faith in a hypnotist, even though
both activities involve faith. Although there are
superficial similarities between hypnosis and many
other activities, it does not follow that they are all the
same.

4

Can the Will
Be Violated?

A primary concern about hypnosis for many people is whether a person's will can be violated through hypnosis. The *Concise Textbook* states:

> A secure ethical value system is important to all therapy and particularly to hypnotherapy, in which patients (especially those in a deep trance) are extremely suggestible and malleable. There is controversy about whether patients will perform acts during a trance state that they otherwise find repugnant or that run contrary to their moral code.[1]

For some experts, will violation is controversial, but other experts state it as a fact. Psychiatrist Arthur Deikman calls the surrender of will "the cardinal feature of the hypnotic state."[2] In their text *Human Behavior*, Berelson and Steiner say, "Not only is a cooperative attitude not necessary for hypnosis, some people can even be hypnotized against their will."[3]

In answering the question, "what are the dangers of hypnosis?" stage hypnotist and entertainer James J. Mapes said:

> Like any other science, it can be, and is, abused. Once the hypnotist has gained your trust, he or she has an obligation not to abuse it, for the hypnotist can induce both positive and negative hallucinations while the subject is hypnotized. That is, the hypnotist can make a subject "see" that which is not there, as in a mirage, or can take away something that is there, such as psychosomatic blindness. For another example, the hypnotist could give a person a real gun and through suggestion tell the subject it was a water pistol and suggest that the subject squirt his or her friend. This is a dramatic example, but certainly possible.[4]

This would certainly constitute will violation through trickery.

Dr. David Spiegel, a Stanford University professor in the school of medicine, says:

> The common idea that you would never do anything in hypnosis that you would not ordinarily do is not in fact true. You are more vulnerable and more at risk in a trance state because you are more focused in your attention and you are not as likely to think about peripheral considerations like is this a good idea to do this or what am I really doing?[5]

Nevertheless, it is essential for the hypnotist to sustain the notion of will control on the part of the patient. The patient will more easily trust a hypnotist if he is assured that his will is not being violated and that he can exercise free choice at any time during a trance. If hypnosis could cause a person to do something against his will and if the trance state could open up such a possibility, then hypnotism should be considered repugnant to Christians.

Divided Will Control

The process of hypnosis brings about a type of dissociation in which the individual retains choice (referred to as *executive control)* in certain areas while at the same time he submits other areas of choice to the hypnotist. Thus, during hypnosis an individual may feel in control of himself because he can still make many choices. For instance, in experimental hypnosis where persons had the freedom to move about as *they* chose, they hallucinated according to the hypnotist's suggestions. Thus during hypnosis there is a division of control. While the hypnotized persons retain numerous areas of choice, they have turned some areas of choice over to the hypnotist. Hilgard says of the subjects, "Within the hypnotic contract, they will do what the hypnotist suggests, experience what they are told to experience, and lose control of movements."[6] For example, when the subject is told that he cannot move his arm, he will not be able to move his arm.

Margaretta Bowers tells how "the perception of the world of outer reality fades away . . . and there comes a time when the voice of the hypnotist is heard as if within the subject's own mind, and he responds to the will of the hypnotist as to his own will."[7]

Another area of the will surrendered during hypnosis is the *monitoring function*. The monitoring function helps us make decisions by comparing past situations with the current situation. Such recall of information and application to the present situation may change our decision on how to act, such as: "If I run around making noises and acting like a monkey, I will look like a fool." With such monitoring functions impaired, an individual may perform acts which he would not even consider otherwise.

Since reality becomes distorted during a trance, the subject cannot properly evaluate which actions make sense and which ones do not. Hilgard says that in the trance state there is a trance logic that accepts "what would normally be found incompatible."[8] Thus, an individual within the hypnotic trance may flap his arms up and down in response to a hypnotist's suggestion that he has wings. If reality is distorted and the person is not able to make reality judgments, his means of responsible choice have been impaired. He is unable to exercise his own will responsibly.

The exercise of choice and the use of information during a person's normal state are distorted during hypnosis and may result in the individual releasing some of these areas to the hypnotist. If one does not retain his complete normal capacity to evaluate reality and to choose, then it appears that his will could be intruded upon and at least partially violated. A well-known textbook of psychiatry states:

> Hypnosis can be described as an altered state of intense and sensitive interpersonal relatedness between hypnotist and patient, characterized by the patient's nonrational submission and relative

abandonment of executive control to a more or less regressed, dissociated state.[9]

Although this interference with choice and reality testing may be temporary, there is the possibility of post-hypnotic suggestion which would remain as an influence and also the possibility of further dissociation of these functions.

It is apparent to us that a hypnotist *can* deceive a person into committing an act which would be in violation of his normal range of choice.[10] A hypnotist can even lead a person into committing murder by creating an extreme fear that someone is attempting to kill him. The patient would discern it as an act of self-defense. Through hypnotic deception, it is possible to cause one to do something against his will by disguising the act into one which would be within his choice.

Since a person under hypnosis would do something if it is made plausible and desirable, and since reality is distorted under hypnosis, violation can occur through the fact that the subject is in a more highly suggestible state and the trance propagator can make almost anything plausible and desirable. Hypnotist Simeon Edmunds cites numerous cases in his book *Hypnotism and Psychic Phenomena* to illustrate his belief that it is possible for a hypnotist to perform an illegal act against a subject and that it is even possible for a hypnotist to cause a subject to perform an illegal act.[11]

Aside from the calm assurances from hypnotherapists that a person's will is not violated under hypnosis there is little proof that it cannot be violated. The subject of will violation is not only controversial, but is complicated by the fact that it is impossible to know completely what a person's true will is in all circumstances. A man may say, "I love my mother-in-law," but actually hate her. The question of violation of the will may not lend itself to solution by rhetoric or by research because of its complicated nature.[12]

In his book *"R.F.K. Must Die!" A History of the Robert Kennedy Assassination and Its Aftermath,* Robert Blair Kaiser raises the question of the accused, Sirhan Sirhan, having been hypnotized beforehand and being in a trance when he killed Kennedy. Kaiser says:

> According to a widely accepted cliché, propagated in the main by stage hypnotists and others who have commercial interest in hypnosis, no one can be induced through hypnosis to do anything against his own moral code. The history of hypnosis, however, and the annals of crime itself are proof enough that skilled operators can lead certain highly suggestible subjects to do "bad" things by corrupting their sense of reality and appealing to some "higher morality."
>
> On July 17, 1954, Bjorn Schouw Nielsen was convicted in Copenhagen Central Criminal Court and sentenced to life imprisonment for "having planned and instigated by influence of various kinds, including suggestions of a hypnotic nature," the commission of two robberies and two murders by another man. This man, Palle Hardrup, is free today because Dr. Paul Reiter, chief of the psychiatric department of the Copenhagen Municipal Hospital, spent nineteen months on an exhaustive study of the weird—possibly homosexual—

relationship between the two men, which began in prison years before.

According to Dr. Reiter, Nielsen created a blindly obedient instrument in Hardrup, who would go into a trance at the sound (or the sight) of a simple signal—the letter X—and do whatever Nielsen suggested. Nielsen convinced Hardrup, in hypnosis, that he was a chosen instrument for the unification of all Scandinavia. Hardrup would form a new political party, would work under the direction of a guardian spirit—X—(who would communicate to him through Nielsen). Once this attitude was instilled, Nielsen induced Hardrup to raise money for the new party by robbing banks (and turning the money over to Nielsen). Hardrup robbed one bank successfully, and then, in the course of another, he killed a teller and a director of the bank and was arrested soon afterward by Copenhagen police.

It was Reiter's conclusion that Nielsen had created in Hardrup a split personality, a paranoid schizophrenic, who was never aware, until Reiter's work with him, that he had been programmed for crime, and programmed to forget that he had been programmed. Reiter's complete account is a chilling tale of mysticism and murder—and of some very persistent detective work by Reiter perhaps unparalleled in the history of psychiatry and crime.

So it was not impossible. Sirhan could have been programmed and programmed to forget.[13]

Because hypnosis places responsibility outside the exercise of objective, rational, fully conscious choice, it does violate the will. The normal evaluating abilities are submerged and choice is made according to suggestion without the balance of rational restraint.

The will is a precious treasure of humans and shows forth the indelible hand of our Creator. The human will requires more respect than hypnosis seems to offer. Bypassing the responsible state of reason and choice just because of the hope for some desired end is bad medicine and, worst of all, bad theology. Because of this, we add the possibility of will violation to the list of reasons why Christians should be wary of hypnosis.

5

Induction/Seduction

Pierre Janet, an early practitioner of modern hypnotherapy, had no qualms about deceiving his patients into a trance. He clearly declared:

> There are some patients to whom . . . we must tell part of the truth; and there are some to whom, as a matter of strict moral obligation, we must lie.[1]

These startling words call us to take a closer look at hypnosis and how it is being used today. Let's start at the beginning. What happens when a hypnotist begins hypnotizing someone?

Hypnosis begins with creative manipulation. A hypnotist leads an individual into a state of hypnosis through a process called *induction*. The hypnotherapist uses techniques such as repetition, deception, stimulation of the imagination, and emotionally overtoned suggestions to effectively influence the will and condition the behavior of the subject.[2]

Few people realize that hypnotic induction often involves subtle forms of deception. Even if a hypnotist attempts to make only true and honest statements, deception may enter in through the distortion of reality which begins during induction and continues throughout the hypnotic trance.

Dr. Keith Harary says: "The ambiguity surrounding what it means to be under the influence of hypnosis starts right at the beginning, with no standard for hypnotic induction."[3]

In her book *Creative Scripts for Hypnotherapy*, Dr. Marlene Hunter says:

> There are surely as many induction techniques in hypnosis as there are people who practice hypnosis—indeed, many times that number, for almost everyone has several—and it would obviously be impossible even to describe all the main categories.[4]

Hunter gives examples of only three types of induction techniques—Basic Techniques, Visual Imagery, and Eye-Fixation. In each of these techniques Hunter gives both the words to say and the timing to use. The following is only a part of the "Basic Induction Techniques" she uses:

> By and by you may find your eyes getting just a little heavier and it seems as if it would be nice to let them close for a little while. Find out how it feels to let them close for a few seconds and then open them again—then close open one more time and close—that's right. You may notice that there is a gentle flickering in your eyelids. That can be a cue for you, that you are entering some delightful space in your mind where time loses its usual

meaning and you are able to perceive so many things in a different way.[5]

Next to these words to be spoken to the subject about closing the eyes, Hunter adds this note: "less intimidating than the suggestion to close them—period—especially in an inexperienced subject." Next to the words about flickering eyelids, she adds the note: "if you watch carefully, you will see the eyes glaze just before they flicker—a good time to mention it!"[6] Later in the words to be spoken to the subject, Hunter provides the following:

And while you are doing that, your inner mind will be taking you to your own best level of comfortable hypnosis, whatever is just right for you, to achieve what you are going to achieve today.[7]

The idea she says she wants to communicate to the subject is that whatever YOU (the subject) do, is right.[8]

At the end of her section on the "Eye Fixation Technique" Hunter provides the following script for the hypnotherapist to speak to the subject:

Later on, when you learn to do your own hypnosis, you can use it as a signal to yourself—that you are just ready to go into that very pleasant state. Some people find that it will persist; for others, it eases away quite quickly; for many, it seems to come and go, probably depending on changing levels in hypnosis, but it's almost always there to begin with. So you can think of it as a nice clue, that you are just entering that very pleasant state.[9]

Hunter's notes next to the above script are: "this is your tool" and "whatever happens is the right thing to happen." These notes, including the ones about flickering eyelids, are examples of the way hypnotists anticipate and manipulate responses and motivate the subject to go into a trance.

Hunter advises the hypnotist to: "State and restate several times that whatever happens is the right thing to happen at any hypnotic experience."[10] The plan is to tailor what is said to each individual to increase confidence in the hypnotist and the process, to lower the individual's resistance, and to encourage the subject into a trance state. It is a deceptive and dishonest use of words in order to overcome resistance and to ease the subject into a trance state.

At the very beginning of the session Hunter advises:

> The preamble is also a good time to implant positive suggestions such as "I can see that you are well motivated, and that is the most important quality for a successful hypnotic experience."[11]

This is a lie used to lower the subject's resistance and increase his motivation to cooperate.

If resistance occurs on the part of the subject, Hunter advises the hypnotist:

> The first opportunity to defuse resistance comes when you are explaining to inexperienced subjects about hypnosis in general, remarking that resistance is normal and even to be desired. It is a signal that their wise, deep, inner mind is taking care of them.[12]

This is another example of hypnotists' dishonest use of words to lower resistance through the use of an unsubstantiated compliment.

Hunter gives a number of suggestions to overcome resistance and to obtain cooperation. Notice the manipulation of words in the following two examples:

> Many people will state, rather belligerently, "I can NEVER relax." The response to that is to say, quickly, "Oh, please DO NOT relax! Simply enjoy listening to my voice. You are one of those people who will do their best work when they are *listening closely*, and *focusing* on what I am saying." We know that the subconscious mind tends to disregard the negatives and "please DO NOT . . ." will be interpreted as "please DO. . . ."
>
> For those subjects who keep their eyes open the happy comment, "Oh, you are one of those people who like to *go into hypnosis with your eyes open*," will usually result in an immediate closing of the eyes.[13]

The *Concise Textbook* also gives advice for trance induction:

> The therapist can use a number of specific procedures to help the patient be hypnotized and respond to suggestion. Those procedures involve capitalizing on some naturally occurring hypnosislike phenomena that have probably occurred in the life experiences of most patients. However, those experiences are rarely talked about; consequently, patients find them fascinating. For example, when discussing what hypnosis

is like with a patient, the therapist may say: "Have you ever had the experience of driving home while thinking about an issue that preoccupies you and suddenly realize that, although you have arrived safe and sound, you can't recall having driven past familiar landmarks? It's as if you had been asleep, and yet you stopped at all the red lights, and you avoided collisions. You were somehow traveling on automatic pilot." Most people resonate to that experience and are usually happy to describe similar personal experiences.[14]

The authors admit that this episode is not necessarily an hypnotic state but it is used so that the subject might correlate it to hypnotizability. Obviously this is a deception to gain an advantage, which might make the subject feel that hypnosis is as safe as what he has already experienced and thereby open him up to a trance state. The authors of the *Concise Textbook* are aware that many experts would not regard the above episode as a trance state.

One form of deception employed by hypnotists is double-bind suggestions. Medical doctor William Kroger and psychologist William Fezler, two well-known authorities on hypnosis, describe induction by saying that it "consists of a sequential series of double-bind suggestions."[15] Double-bind suggestions are comments made to the subject to indicate that his response (no matter what it is) is an appropriate one for moving into the state of hypnosis. The suggestions are arranged to elicit the subject's confidence and cooperation so that he may relax. Kroger and Fezler suggest such things as:

If the patient's eyes blink or the individual swallows one can say, "See, you just blinked," or swallowed, as the case may be. These act as reinforcers to suggest that the patient is doing fine.[16]

Other such reinforcements are used by Kroger and Fezler to lead the person more quickly into the trance. Milton Erickson, known as the "grand master of clinical hypnosis," used the double-bind to give his patients a pseudochoice. The patient could choose a light trance or a deep trance but, either way, the patient ended up in a trance.[17] Hypnotherapist Peter Francuch says, "It is very important to utilize every reaction of the client to deepen his trance."[18]

Kroger and Fezler discuss a number of other "factors influencing hypnotic induction," including the prestige of the therapist. They say:

A therapist who is in a "one up" position commands respect from the supplicant who is in a "one down" position. If the latter regards the therapist with awe and respect, particularly if he is an authority, the prestige increases success of the hypnotic induction.[19]

Pierre Janet speaks even more dramatically of the domination of the subject by the hypnotist. He says:

The relationship of a hypnotizable patient to the hypnotist does not differ in any essential way from the relationship of a lunatic to the superintendent of an asylum.[20]

After induction, deception may continue, depending upon the purposes of the trance. During experimental hypnosis, subjects are sometimes told that they will be temporarily deaf. And they indeed will not hear anything even though there are noises and voices in the room.[21] Is this merely suggestion or is it deception? Another experiment consists of telling the subjects that they will see a clock with a missing hour hand. When the clock is shown to them, they hallucinate and see what they are told to see: a clock without an hour hand, even though the clock is intact. Professor Ernest Hilgard says, "With critical abilities reduced, imagination readily becomes hallucination."[22] Thus, **through deception subjects hallucinate according to suggestion**.

Janet admitted that hypnosis rests upon deception. Responding to the moral objection of a hypnotist deceiving his patient, he said:

> I am sorry that I cannot share these exalted and beautiful scruples. . . . My belief is that the patient wants a doctor who will cure; that the doctor's professional duty is to give any remedy that will be useful, and to prescribe it in the way in which it will do most good.[23]

Hypnotic induction, therefore, consists of a system of verbal and nonverbal manipulation to lead a person into a heightened state of suggestibility—more simply, a condition in which one will believe almost anything.

Hypnosis and Deception:
From Suggestion to Placebo

Professor of psychiatry Thomas Szasz emphasizes that hypnosis is the power of suggestion.[24] Research psychiatrist E. Fuller Torrey asks and then answers a question which supports this point of view:

> How can witchdoctors, relying primarily on such techniques as suggestion and hypnosis, achieve as good results as Western therapists who use techniques so much more sophisticated?[25]

Torrey first replies that Western techniques are not actually more sophisticated at all and that "we consistently underestimate the power of techniques like suggestion and hypnosis."[26]

Kroger declares, "The power of hypnosis is the power of belief!" and identifies hypnosis as a form of faith healing. He says:

> The question as to whether religious or hypnotic faith healing is more effective obviously relates to previous conditioning of the subject.[27]

In examining hypnotism, we have found it referred to as a form of suggestion, as faith, and finally as the placebo effect. The placebo effect takes place when one has faith in a certain person, or a prescribed pill, or a procedure; it is this faith that brings about the healing. The person, pill, or procedure may be fake, but the result may be real. Janet saw the relationship between hypnosis and the fake pill. To defend the value of deception in hypnosis, he cited his belief in the placebo and stressed that he was fulfilling his "professional duty" when he prescribed a fake pill with faith-producing statements.[28]

Kroger and others also confess that hypnosis involves the placebo effect. Kroger and Fezler say that "faith in a specific cure leads to the success of that cure!"[29] Kroger also says, "Every psychotherapist owes it to his patients to utilize his unquestioned placebo effect at the highest level—hypnosis." Just as the placebo is not effective with all patients, Kroger admits that hypnosis is not successful with all individuals.[30] He concludes, "Our thesis is that if the placebo is effective, then hypnosis employed prudently by a competent physician for a valid indication will serve the patient's best interest."[31]

The placebo effect is not limited to hypnosis. It also works in acupuncture, biofeedback, and generally in psychotherapy. A number of studies support the idea that some mental, emotional, and even physical change is in the mind. A study of the use of acupuncture at one university indicates that the patient's expectation of relief can influence the results. The researchers found that acupuncture works best on those people who exhibit faith in the procedure. Positive remarks that the experimenters made to the patients encouraged higher expectations. Their conclusion: for acupuncture to reduce pain it had to be accompanied by words and actions which would help the patient to believe that the treatment would be successful.[32]

Other studies have shown that a variety of anxiety and stress symptoms can be reduced by giving false information to subjects. To illustrate the power of faith and the placebo effect, one researcher showed how false feedback can reduce symptoms of cardiovascular disease. In this experiment the subjects were told that their test results were improving, even though they were not. Through the use of false feedback with biofeedback devices, patients received a sense of self-control. As the false feedback communicated increasing levels of success, the patients believed that they had greater self-control. Over a period of weeks the subjects reported a decrease in stress symptoms.[33] One reason for such improvements is a person's faith in his own natural powers. Thus, "biofeedback training may be . . . an 'ultimate placebo.'"[34]

Another study reported that false information about room temperature can influence body comfort. The study showed that "misinforming people about room temperature can lead them to feel warmer or cooler than they might if they knew the actual temperature."[35]

Psychiatrist Arthur Shapiro states that "psycho-analysis—and its dozens of psychotherapy offshoots—is the most used placebo of our time."[36] One form of psychotherapy, Social Influence Therapy, purposely uses false feedback in order to achieve success. One practitioner of this brand of therapy says:

> Humanitarian fervor aside, it's the therapist's job to take power over the patient, push ahead with solving the problem, then convince the patient he or she is better, even if it means being devious.[37]

This therapist claims, "Successful therapy can almost be reduced to a formula." The main part of the formula is to convince the "client that the therapy is definitely working apart from any objective evidence of change."[38] In this form of therapy, flattery, distortion, lies, and all forms of what is euphemistically called "false feedback" are used successfully. Ethics aside, this form of therapy is solid testimony to the power of the mind for self transformation.

Any technique or method which depends on deception should be regarded with great suspicion. Hypnosis, along with other questionable "medical" procedures, relies heavily on faith-building devices, including both direct and indirect deception. Can a hypnotist, who uses subtle forms of deception as a means of hypnotizing an individual, be trusted during the trance or even in his assurances of the safety of hypnosis?

6

Age Regression and Progression

Age regression is a common procedure in hypnosis, because so many people erroneously believe that hypnosis will help a person recover forgotten memories or details from vague memories. Mark Twain once said, "I find the further back I go, the better I remember things, whether they happened or not."[1] And this is exactly what can happen in age regression—clearly remembering things that never happened or erroneous details of what may have happened.

Dr. Michael Yapko defines *age regression* this way:

> "Age regression" is a hypnotic procedure in which the client is immersed in the experience of memory. The client may be encouraged to *remember* events in vivid detail, a procedure called "hypermnesia." Or, the client may be encouraged to *relive* the events of the past as if they were going on right now, a procedure called "revivification." Either or

both of these procedures are commonly used in memory recovery-oriented therapies.[2]

The Handbook of Hypnotic Phenomena in Psychotherapy (*The Handbook*) says, "Hypnotic age regression entails a therapist using hypnosis to facilitate a client's going back, experientially, to an earlier time in life."[3] The *Concise Encyclopedia* says:

> Relived emotional experiences (abreactions) are induced by regressing the patient back to traumatic episodes and then having the patient experience them to the point of physical and emotional exhaustion.[4]

Prenatal Lives

In this highly popular form of hypnosis a person is regressed to an earlier time in his life to remember, and possibly relive, past experiences. Otto Rank, a contemporary of Sigmund Freud, believed that the birth process was the most significant event in early life, and therefore, the source of later anxiety. Hypnosis sometimes leads people back to what they identify as their birth experience and even to their prenatal period of existence in order to cure psychological and physical problems. Using regressive hypnosis as a base, some claim that fetuses in-utero and babies at birth are able to understand the words, attitudes and actions of those around them.

Brain/Mind reports:

> Under the influence of hypnosis and psychotropic drugs many people have recalled pre-natal and birth experiences that related to current

physical and psychological problems: headaches, respiratory disorders, phobias, depression, anxiety. Recalling the experiences frequently relieves or eliminates the symptoms.

A client of San Francisco therapist Jack Downing "relived" a painful fetal memory of rejection while under hypnosis. The memory: When his mother said she was pregnant, her husband was upset and wanted her to get an abortion. He said, "I've been saving to buy a Chrysler." A bitter argument ensued.

The client related his current feelings of insecurity to the father's rejection. . . .

Fetal perception of such events is taken very personally, Downing said. "the knowledge involved in such pre-natal conditioning is extremely literal."[5]

If the fetus understands language prior to birth, why does it take so long for a young child to learn the language? How would a fetus have any concept of what a Chrysler or an abortion might be?

The same article includes the following report from a medical doctor:

Head pain is frequently associated with birth trauma, said gynecologist David Cheek. Patients' hypnotic recall of painful pressure to the head during birth is often enough to eliminate symptoms of chronic headache, including migraine.

Cheek's patients commonly relate their reported birth experiences to present moods and behavior patterns. Many patients with asthma and emphysema were nearly suffocated during birth.

Ability to recall the details of one's birth under hypnosis is uncanny, Cheek said. His patients can correctly indicate which arm freed first during delivery and which way the head turned as it emerged. He has verified the accuracy of such reports by checking them against obstetrical notes made during delivery.[6]

Brain/Mind states that up to the age of twenty-three, individuals "under hypnosis accurately report their birth experiences." The report goes on to say that the information derived under hypnosis "corresponds to the mother's recounting of specifics, such as her hairstyle, the obstetric instruments used, conversations in the delivery room, the character and behavior of nurses and doctors, and the mother's own emotional and physical state."[7]

However, this all flies in the face of the well-known, neurological, scientific fact that the myelin sheathing is too underdeveloped in the prenatal, natal, and early postnatal brain to store such memories. David Chamberlain, a San Diego psychologist, paradoxically reports that people "can indeed remember their own births in extraordinary detail" through hypnosis, but that the birth memory is *not* stored in the brain.[8] This raises a question: If memories are not stored in the brain, where are they stored? What might be the source?

Francuch, in his book *Principles of Spiritual Hypnosis,* explains the hypnotically revived natal, prenatal, and postnatal experiences in spiritual terms. He says:

Since the inner mind is present from the very moment of conception (in a unique combination of

the genes and in God from eternity before individuation), it is obvious that it registers, records,
and understands everything that is happening
from the very moment of conception. And since
the ability to understand language is imprinted
in those genes, and while in God from eternity who
originated language, it is thus ever-present in the
inner mind.[9]

This explanation, if accepted, plunges man into a
spiritual puzzle of metaphysics that explains physical
phenomena (conception, etc.) in spiritual terms that
are *neither* biblical nor scientific. Such spiritual
gibberish can open people up to the quagmire of satanic
influence. However, hypnotherapists who use the
prebirth, birth, or rebirth approach claim relief for
everything from asthma to phobias through this
process.[10] And, desperate people become vulnerable to
the promises.

Past Lives
Some of these same hypnotherapists regress people
to so-called previous lives. This form of enchantment
begins with the hypnotherapist leading a person back
to his early years and then beyond those years, beyond
the womb, beyond conception to what they identify as
a former existence. The patient is encouraged to recall,
recount, and relive past life experiences for the therapist. The description of Helen Wambach's book *Reliving Past Lives: The Evidence Under Hypnosis* reports,
"A noted psychologist presents historically valid data
from over 1,000 past-life recalls that strongly suggest
most of us have lived earlier lives in different bodies."[11]

In their book *Past Lives Therapy,* Morris Netherton
and Nancy Shiffrin report numerous cases of individuals who receive relief from physical and emotional
symptoms through hypnotic regression.[12] Some cases
could come from the imagination or they could be
fabricated during the process of hypnosis through
suggestions made by the hypnotist. However, when
cases of past lives accurately match history, one questions the source of the information.

One man who suffered from migraine headaches
reports the feelings he had when his mother suffered
headaches while he was in her womb. Then he "remem-
bers": In a previous life he was captured by Indians
and leather bands were twisted and tightened around
his head. He describes the intensity of the pain; it
becomes tighter and tighter until his skull snaps and
he is no longer in the body. Later he moves into a
"different life" in which he is an Indian and this time a
metal band is around his head. He is being punished
and tortured until he dies. After several other accounts,
he "recalls" the birth experience of his present life.
Voices are saying that his head is stuck and he feels
metal on his head as he is pulled through the birth
canal. After the fourth session of hypnotic regression,
his migraine headaches vanished.[13]

Psychiatrist Brian L. Weiss, author of *Through Time
Into Healing*, is a proponent of past-life therapy. A
Longevity article reports on his work as follows:

> A recent client—one of more than 200 that
> Weiss has treated with past-life therapy over the
> past 11 years—was a depressed woman in her
> forties. As he does with all regression-therapy
> patients, Weiss hypnotized her and suggested she

could mentally travel back to a different time and place to find the cause of her symptoms.

Under hypnosis, the woman recalled wearing the lacy garb of a nineteenth-century prostitute. She had died, she said, after neglecting her body. After the second session with Weiss (whose typical charge is $150 an hour), she began to shed her depression. Weiss says she realized that she had gained weight in her current life to make herself less attractive, thus protecting herself from sexual advances. After about ten sessions, she was exercising regularly and losing weight.[14]

While under hypnosis, Elizabeth Howard, a respected pharmaceutical researcher, recounted details of her "former life." As Elizabeth Fitton she had supposedly lived during the reigns of Queen Mary and Queen Elizabeth I of England. She told about illegitimate births that would not have been public information. She accurately described the interior of the house in which the woman had lived, even though she herself had never been inside.[15] Although many use such accounts to support the notion of reincarnation, such vivid "memories" could easily come from demonic spirits influencing the mind during hypnosis.

Some individuals, either voluntarily or by suggestions of the therapist, even "remember" a previous life on another planet. Paul Bannister reports on a massive five-year study of over 6,000 individuals who underwent hypnosis. He says, "One-fifth described earlier existences on other planets." Bannister concludes, "More than 45 million Americans have lived previous lives on other planets."[16]

Through past lives therapy, the authors of one book claim "to reveal the cause of traumas and problems from sexual inadequacies to phobias to stuttering and migraine headaches, and deal with them effectively."[17] The beneficial effects of past lives therapy are tempting, but the God of the Bible has said, "It is appointed unto men once to die" (Heb. 9:27). It is obvious to most Christians that past lives therapy is demonic, but how much does early life hypnotherapy open up an individual to the power of the Prince of Darkness? And, how far back should a Christian permit himself to be regressed before the danger point is reached? What would a Christian hypnotherapist do if a hypnotized person moved from an early memory to a so-called past life or life on another planet?

Age Progression and Future Lives

Besides past life hypnotic therapy, some practitioners are doing future life hypnotic therapy.[18] In this activity, persons are supposedly hypnotized into the future. According to descriptive reports, the hypnotherapist guides these individuals into future places and future times. The hypnotized person supposedly sees future events, solves murders, and reveals the future fate of well-known personalities. Kroger has pointed out that the great therapeutic value of age progression or future life hypnotherapy is to see how the subject may react in future situations.[19]

According to *Omni* magazine, past-life therapist Bruce Goldberg has:

... performed future-life progressions on over 2,000 people and reports that their descriptions of the future are in agreement about 80 percent of the time. According to his subjects, world peace will come in the twenty-first century, but political strife in the twenty-third century will result in a small-scale nuclear war. By the twenty-fifth century we will control the weather, and androids will perform all menial tasks. But it isn't until the twenty-sixth century that we make contact with beings from other planets.[20]

The Handbook discusses how two authors of an age-progression article dealt with two separate cases. In one case, a woman wished to die and to be reunited with her recently deceased husband in heaven. In the other case a woman "promised a dying person that she would be with the person before very long" and "felt a commitment to the promise" after the person died.[21] *The Handbook* reports:

> With these cases, the authors reported that they first age regressed patients back to the point where the initial promise or death wish took place. Once the nature of the patient's self-perceived transgression or commitment was discovered, they were age progressed *into heaven*, where of their own accord they engaged in conversations with the lost loved ones or with Jesus Christ himself. In the patients' conversations with the loved ones, they worked through the promises that they had made and had the chance to see that the person was doing well. In their conversations with Jesus, they would hear that they were understood, forgiven, and that it was not their time to be in heaven. This was a strikingly imaginative technique, and one that

the authors reported being so highly effective that the psychoses improved dramatically, the depressions lifted quickly, and ego functioning improved significantly.[22]

Please note that besides deception and lies, the sin of necromancy (communication with the dead) is committed during such hypnotic sessions.

On a variation of future-lives therapy, *Longevity* reports:

> Lawrence Casler, Ph.D., professor emeritus at the State University of New York at Geneseo, recruited 100 students into a lifelong study 20 years ago. He hypnotized them, telling one group that they could live to be "at least 120 and probably well beyond that." The others got no hypnotic suggestion relating to longevity. Twice a year, Casler sends his subjects, who are now about 40, questionnaires asking about their general health and life-style. So far, longevity hypnosis seems to be working.[23]

Francuch explains past, present and future experiences in the hypnotic state as follows:

> Such terms as "past," "present," and "future" are irrelevant and meaningless at the spiritual level, and they are replaced by corresponding states, conditions, and occurrences without any dependency on time or space elements.[24]

Francuch describes some experiments in which he participated involving "the plenary state of hypnosis." He says:

The person in the plenary state was able to defy space and time. The person was able very precisely to describe in minute detail what was happening in another friend's house 300 miles away. At the same time, the person was able to describe exactly what was happening a month ago, a year ago, and ten years ago at the same place, and paradoxically, the person was able to describe exactly what was going to happen in the same place the next day, one month from then, and one year from then, etc.[25]

In this hypnotic time travel, where is the line of demarcation between the demonic and the medical, between the realm of Satan and science? At what point does the door of darkness open and the devil gain a foothold?

7

Hypnotic Memory

The most important factor in early life or past life hypnotherapy is memory. Hilgard says, "No matter how one dips into the recesses of the mind, one stumbles on the same problems – the storage and retrieval of information, some true, some false."[1] From examining the research on memory, social psychologist Carol Tavris concludes:

Memory is, in a word, lousy. It is a traitor at worst, a mischief-maker at best. It gives us vivid recollections of events that could never have happened, and it obscures critical details of events that did.[2]

The *Harvard Mental Health Letter* states:

In reality, all memory is a reconstruction rather than a reproduction, and it is almost always deeply unreliable, threaded with fabrications and distortions. Hypnosis multiplies and magnifies the occasions for errors of recollection. Hypnotic subjects readily confuse real with imaginary events and at the same time become overconfident about their memories.[3]

People have devised various experimental situations to examine the authenticity of hypnotically aided memory. One such experiment involved eyewitnesses responding to "a lineup recognition task and a structured recall task." What the researchers found was that:

> Relative to a normal-state control group, subjects responding under the influence of hypnosis were significantly less accurate on both tasks. Heightened susceptibility to misleading implications was shown to be the major source of hypnotic inferiority.[4]

In his book *They Call It Hypnosis*, Baker says, "Confabulation shows up without fail in nearly every context in which hypnosis is employed."[5] Confabulation is the tendency to remember past events to be different from the way they actually were and even to remember fantasized events as having actually happened. Even ordinary people, who are not under the influence of hypnosis, will have to recreate a memory, especially if they need to remember details of past events. Memory is not like a tape-recorder with all details remembered; instead one has to reconstruct past events. Baker refers to the song "I Remember It Well" in the movie *Gigi*, in which a husband and wife have distinctively different memories of their courtship and says:

> We remember things not the way they really were. . . . We blur, shape, erase, and change details of

the events in our past. Many people walk around with their heads full of "fake memories." Moreover, the unreliability of eye-witness testimony is not only legendary but well documented. When all of this is further complicated and compounded by the impact of suggestions provided by the hypnotist, as well as the social-demand characteristics of the typical hypnotic situation, it is little wonder that the resulting recall bears slight resemblance to the truth.[6]

Memory expert Dr. Elizabeth Loftus declares, "There's no way even the most sophisticated hypnotist can tell the difference between a memory that is real and one that's created."[7]

The Council on Scientific Affairs of the American Medical Association reports:

> The Council finds that recollections obtained during hypnosis can involve confabulations and pseudomemories and not only fail to be more accurate, but actually appear to be less reliable than nonhypnotic recall. The use of hypnosis with witnesses and victims may have serious consequences for the legal process when testimony is based on material that is elicited from a witness who has been hypnotized for the purposes of refreshing recollection.[8]

Regarding memory, the Council says:

> The assumption, however, that a process analogous to a multichannel videotape recorder inside the head records all sensory impressions and

stores them in their pristine form indefinitely is not consistent with research findings or with current theories of memory.[9]

Many people believe that hypnosis enables people to remember things that they have forgotten and that are outside conscious memory or awareness. However, it is now well known that when hypnotic memories are objectively examined, many are false and some are total fabrications. In discussing hypnotic age regression, Baker says:

> Confabulations, i.e., making up stories to fill in memory gaps, seemed to be the norm rather than the exception. It seems, literally, that using "hypnosis" to revive or awaken a person's past history somehow or other not only stimulates the person's desire to recall and his memory processes, but it also opens the flood gates of his or her imagination. Everything the person has experienced, seen, heard, or read seems to suddenly become available and is woven into a comprehensive and credible story. A story that, in many cases, the teller or narrator is convinced is something that actually happened.[10]

The best-selling book *The Search for Bridey Murphy*, published in 1956, was a boon for hypnotic regression. The book tells about an amateur hypnotist hypnotizing a woman who, under hypnosis, became a woman who had lived about 150 years earlier. Bridey Murphy's story about her life in Ireland was supposedly revealed through numerous hypnotic sessions. Many people believed this story proved that hypnosis could enable people to remember events completely outside their own conscious memory.[11]

Of course there have been critiques and exposés of the Bridey Murphy claims as well as other books making similar claims. Nevertheless such books have influenced people's beliefs about both hypnosis and reincarnation. Baker says:

> All of these books either accept reincarnation as a fact, or maintain in a pseudoneutral manner that a belief in reincarnation is lent additional credence by the material uncovered by way of hypnotic regression.[12]

The *Orlando Sentinel* reports that "according to a 1990 Gallop poll, 21 percent of Americans believe in reincarnation."[13]

Therapists who encourage memory work in therapy may actually be leading clients into a trance state without realizing it. Others who have a narrow definition of hypnosis may actually deny using hypnosis, when in fact they are. Michael Yapko, a psychologist and author of *Trancework*, which is a widely-used text, says:

> Many times therapists aren't even aware that they're doing hypnosis. They're doing what they call guided imagery or guided meditation, which are all very mainstream hypnotic techniques.[14]

No matter how memories are accessed, the following statements from "Recovered memories: Are They Reliable?"[15] should be kept in mind:

"The use of recovered memories is fraught with problems of potential misapplication." The American Medical Association, Council on Scientific Affairs, *Memories of Childhood Sexual Abuse*, 1994.

"It is not known how to distinguish, with complete accuracy, memories based on true events from those derived from other sources." American Psychiatric Association, Statement on Memories of Sexual Abuse, 1993.

"The available scientific and clinical evidence does not allow accurate, inaccurate, and fabricated memories to be distinguished in the absence of independent corroboration." Australian Psychological Society, *Guidelines Relating to the Reporting of Recovered Memories*, 1994.

"At this point it is impossible, without other corroborative evidence, to distinguish a true memory from a false one." American Psychological Association, *Questions and Answers about Memories of Childhood Abuse*, 1995.

"Psychologists acknowledge that a definite conclusion that a memory is based on objective reality is not possible unless there is incontrovertible corroborating evidence." Canadian Psychological Association, *Position Statement on Adult Recovered Memories of Childhood Sexual Abuse*, 1996.

"Research has shown that over time memory for events can be changed or reinterpreted in such a way as to make the memory more consistent with the person's present knowledge and/or expectations." American Psychological Association, 1995.

An article in the *Calgary Herald* describes the complexities of memory reconstruction very well. It says:

Recently, courts have become embroiled in debates over the validity of amnesia claims, recovered memories, false-memory syndrome and other quirks of the human mind.

We all know the paths long-ago events take in our memories. They fade and we pick up the crayons and colour them in again a little brighter than before and in slightly different hues. The edges unravel and we embroider them anew. Faces blur, events jumble and rearrange themselves, the timbre of voices heard long ago is lost forever and when we try to pin down distant details they dissolve into shimmery pools of doubt.

Remembering is not a simple straightforward act. It is reconstruction, and in that subconscious tearing down and building up, events are altered and scenes subtly shift. Some memories are erased, others created.[16]

Yes, memories can even be created, not from remembering true events, but by implanting imagined events into the mind. In fact, it is possible for implanted and enhanced memories to seem even more vivid than memories of actual past events. Under certain condi-

tions a person's mind is open to suggestion in such a
way that illusions of memory can be received, believed,
and remembered as true memories. Exploring the past
through conversation, counseling, hypnosis, guided
imagery, and regressive therapy **is as likely to cause
a person to create false memories as to remember accurate accounts of past situations**. In a state
of heightened suggestibility a person's memory can
easily be altered and enhanced.

Bernard Diamond, a professor of law and a clinical
professor of psychiatry, says that court witnesses who
have been hypnotized "often develop a certitude about
their memories that ordinary witnesses seldom
exhibit."[17] Diamond states that hypnotized persons
"graft onto their memories fantasies or suggestions
deliberately or unwittingly communicated by the
hypnotist." Diamond then reveals that "after hypnosis
the subject cannot differentiate between a true recollection and a fantasy or a suggested detail."[18] Thus the
hypnotized subject does not even know he is fabricat-
ing. In examining memory and the use of hypnosis,
the California Supreme Court concluded that "the
memory does not act like a video tape recorder, but
rather is subject to numerous influences that continu-
ously alter its contents."[19] One might say that memory
is guilty by reason of humanity.

Research shows that hypnosis is just as likely to
dredge up false information as true accounts of past
events.[20] In addition, studies have shown that individuals *can* and *do* lie under hypnosis.[21] Because memory
is so unreliable, any method of cure which relies upon
memory is generally unreliable. The certainty of
pseudomemories and the uncertainty of real memo-

ries render hypnosis a questionable practice when memory is involved in the cure.

Diamond asks and answers a number of questions about hypnosis in the *California Law Review*. Some of the questions and portions of their answers follow:

> Can a hypnotized person be free from heightened suggestibility? The answer is no. Hypnosis is, almost by definition, a state of increased suggestibility.
>
> Can a hypnotist, through the exercise of skill and attention, avoid implanting suggestions in the mind of the hypnotized subject? No, such suggestions cannot be avoided.
>
> After awakening, can the hypnotic subject consistently recognize which of his thoughts, feelings, and memories were his own and which were implanted by the hypnotic experience? No. It is very difficult for human beings to recognize that some of their own thoughts might have been implanted and might not be the product of their own volition.
>
> Is it rare for a subject to believe that he was not hypnotized when in fact he was? No. On the contrary, very often hypnotic subjects refuse to believe they actually went into a trance.
>
> Can previously hypnotized persons restrict their memory to actual facts, free from fantasies and confabulations? No. . . . Out of a desire to comply with the hypnotist's suggestions, the subject will

commonly fill in missing details by fantasy or
confabulation.

After the hypnotic subject is awakened, do the
distorting effects of the hypnosis disappear? The
evidence . . . is that the effect of suggestions made
during hypnosis endures.

During or after hypnosis, can the hypnotist or
the subject himself sort out fact from fantasy in
the recall? Again the answer is no. No one,
regardless of experience, can verify the accuracy
of the hypnotically enhanced memory.[22]

The above information should have an extremely
sobering effect upon anyone interested in using
hypnosis. How many of these possibilities affect a
hypnotized person even if the sole purpose of the
hypnosis is pain relief, sleep enhancement, sexual
adjustment, or any one of the hundreds of promises
associated with hypnotism?

8

Deep Hypnosis

Professor of psychology Charles Tart spent much laboratory time investigating hypnosis. He reports an experiment measuring hypnotic depth with a man whom he identifies as William. He recorded the experiences of William, an intelligent, well-adjusted twenty-year-old college student.[1] After hypnotizing William a few times to explore hypnotic depth, he asked William to indicate the various depths while under hypnosis. William and Tart assigned numbers to these depths; we will merely report the various effects. The first was a sense of relaxation and then a separation from his physical body, which William referred to as "just a thing, something I've left behind." His vision was affected and he sensed a blackness which progressively became more intense. He felt peaceful until peacefulness was no longer a "meaningful concept . . . there is no longer a self to be peaceful or not peaceful beyond this point." Along with these other sensations, William moved through various degrees of awareness of his environment and his identity.[2]

Through the earlier stages William was aware of himself, but then his identity became "centered in his head." Later he felt that he was no longer just himself, but something much more: *"potential to be anything or anyone."* William's sense of time dissolved into a sense of timelessness. At the deeper levels there was "an awareness of some sort of chant or humming sound that [was] identified with the feeling that more and more experience [was] potentially available."

Tart notes, "The chant William reported may be related to the Hindu concept of the sacred syllable Om, supposedly a basic sound of the universe that a man can 'hear' as mind becomes more universally attuned." William's feeling of being one with the universe was definitely similar to a Hindu religious experience. This sense of merging with the universe and losing personal identity, yet having the potential for "anything or anyone," increases more and more as the hypnosis deepens.[3]

Tart concludes his report on his work with William by saying that William moved into stages "similar to Eastern descriptions of consciousness of the void . . . in which time, space, and ego are supposedly transcended, leaving pure awareness of the primal nothingness from which all manifested creation comes." Tart believes that such experiments "raise the possibility of using hypnotic states to induce and/or model mystical states."[4]

At any level of hypnosis there is a distortion of reality. It seems that as the hypnotic trance deepens, the possibility of demonic danger grows. Paradoxically, some claim it is at the deeper levels of hypnosis that the most beneficial work can be done. Daniel Goleman says:

Like meditation and biofeedback, hypnosis can open the way for a person to enter a wide range of discrete states of consciousness, or, more rarely, altered states.[5]

The *Concise Textbook* states categorically that "Trance states are altered states of consciousness."[6] Melvin Gravitz, former president of the American Society of Clinical Hypnotism, calls the trance-like condition an "altered state of consciousness."[7] Erika Fromm, in an article titled "Altered States of Consciousness and Hypnosis," says, "It is time for researchers in altered states of consciousness and in hypnosis to get acquainted with each other, to recognize that hypnosis is an ASC [altered state of consciousness]."[8]

If, indeed hypnosis is an altered state of consciousness and/or a trance, it is also related to shamanism. In her book on shamanism and modern medicine, Dr. Jeanne Achterberg says, "The basis of shamanic work is the trance."[9]

Shaman Michael Harner, in his book *The Way of the Shaman*, describes the similarities between the shamanic state of consciousness and an altered state of consciousness. Harner says, "What *is* definite is that some degree of alteration of consciousness is necessary to shamanic practice."[10] Harner quotes one writer who says:

What we are really trying to establish is that the shaman is in a nonordinary psychic state which in some cases means not a loss of consciousness but rather an altered state of consciousness.[11]

Near the end of his book Harner says:

The burgeoning field of holistic medicine shows a tremendous amount of experimentation involving the reinvention of many techniques long practiced in shamanism, such as visualization, altered state of consciousness, aspects of psychoanalysis, hypnotherapy, meditation, positive attitude, stress-reduction, and mental and emotional expression of personal will for health and healing. In a sense, shamanism is being reinvented in the West precisely because it is needed.[12]

In describing deep hypnosis, Ernest Hilgard says:

Distortions of consciousness occur that have some similarity to the reports of mystical experiences. ... The passage of time becomes meaningless, the body seems to be left behind, a new sense of infinite potentiality emerges, ultimately reaching the sense of oneness with the universe.[13]

In describing experiences at the various levels of the hypnotic trance, clinical psychologist Peter Francuch says:

Up to the five hundredth, one goes through various states and levels that reflect different states and levels of the spiritual world and its conditions. At the 126th level, there is a state that corresponds to the state described by the Eastern mystics.[14]

Francuch has taken subjects far beyond this trance level and describes what happened to a particular subject:

The subject emerged from the 126th state, or state of void, nothingness, Nirvana, as a new-born individual with a high level of individuation, differentiation, and at the same time, absorption of the Universe and creation within and without, being simultaneously one with and different from Creation. This state is impossible to describe in words, because nothing exists in the human vocabulary that corresponds to it.

He also says:

I was told that once we break the 1,000 level, all laws, rules, and regulations as they are known to all levels of spirituality and the natural world will be broken, and something completely new will appear. [15]

Hypnotic trance at the deeper levels can and usually does result in the above descriptions, which will be easily identified by Christians as occult, but these obvious manifestations of the occult may not appear at the shallow levels. We can only warn that the deeper the induction, the greater the danger; the deeper the trance, the more potential for harm. However, this raises a question: What is the relationship between the various levels of hypnosis and at what level does a person enter the danger zone? Also, considering the Hilgard study of somnambules who easily move into the deeper levels of trance, will any persons who submit themselves to a trance become vulnerable to sexual fantasies or psychic experiences?

Hilgard's description of deep hypnosis refers to "a separation of mind from body, a feeling of oneness with the universe."[16] David Haddon in the *Spiritual Counterfeits Newsletter* warns: "Any technique or practice that alters the consciousness to an empty-minded state of passivity should be avoided." Haddon warns against the production and enhancement of the passive mental state through whatever means and says:

> While those kinds of techniques are often taken up for the supposed psychological and physical benefits rather than as spiritual disciplines, the user's intention will not prevent experience of the passive mental state with its attendant hazards.[17]

Haddon lists the hazards of mindlessness:

> It blinds the mind to the truth of the gospel by displacing reason as a means to truth . . . it opens the mind to false ideas about God and reality. . . opens the personality to demonic incursion.[18]

Haddon's article is primarily about meditation, but we believe that these possibilities apply equally to hypnosis. Kroger says, "For centuries, Zen, Buddhist, Tibetan, and Yogic methods have used a system of meditation and an altered state of consciousness similar to hypnosis."[19]

Hypnotic trance and demonic possession certainly have some things in common. Hilgard describes two cases of trance in which possession was involved. In the first case the individual "becomes possessed by the Monkey God" and in the second case the individual "has a choice of spirits to call on." Hilgard says:

The spirit would possess him and then answer questions, particularly making recommendations for the cure of illness, including the special curative powers of a charmed glass of water.[20]

Does hypnosis act as an invitation to demonic possession? One cult leader, a former professional hypnotist, claims, "Once you've been hypnotized, your mind will never be your own again."[21] While we do not endorse such an extreme statement, there may nonetheless be some truth in it.

Francuch is a perfect example of how a clinical psychologist can proceed from hypnosis to spiritual hypnosis and then to the mystical and the occult. The promotion flyer for his third book, *Messages from Within,* says:

This book consists of thirty-six plus messages received by him from his highest spiritual advisor—the Most High—in the process of his profound spiritual self-hypnosis, meditation and dialogue with his Inner Mind.[22]

The pathway to psychic experiences, demon possession, and who knows what else may indeed be through hypnosis.

9

Hypnosis:
Medical, Scientific,
or Occultic?

The words most used by those who support hypnosis for Christians are *medical* and *scientific*. These words not only provide prestige, but also a feeling of safety. When the word *medical* comes up, the guard goes down. Any practice labeled *medical*, and therefore scientific, is an "open sesame" to the saints. Those who encourage hypnosis for Christians rely upon this questionable label of *science* to support its use. However, Donald Hebb says in "Psychology Today/The State of the Science" that "hypnosis has persistently lacked satisfactory explanation."[1] At the present time there is no agreed-upon scientific explanation of exactly what hypnosis is. Psychiatry professor Thomas Szasz describes hypnosis as the therapy of "a fake science."[2] We cannot call hypnosis a science, but we can say that it has been an integral part of the occult for thousands of years.

E. Fuller Torrey, a research psychiatrist, aligns hypnotic techniques with witchcraft. He also says, "Hypnosis is one aspect of the yoga techniques of therapeutic meditation."[3]

Medical doctor William Kroger states, "The fundamental principles of Yoga are, in many respects, similar to those of hypnosis."[4] To protect the scientific label for hypnosis he declares, "Yoga is not considered a religion, but rather a 'science' to achieve mastery of the mind and cure physical and emotional sickness." Then he makes a strange confession, "There are many systems to Yoga, but the central aim—union with God—is common to all of them and is the method by which it achieves cure."[5]

Many medical doctors use the energy centers of yoga to alleviate physical diseases. Kroger and William Fezler say:

> The reader should not be confused by the supposed differences between hypnosis, Zen, Yoga and other Eastern healing methodologies. Although the ritual for each differs, they are fundamentally the same.[6]

Thus, the word "medical" may include much more than one might suppose. Nevertheless, some in the church have advocated hypnosis as long as it is in the hands of a trained professional, especially a medical doctor. A person who desperately needs help for some long-term difficult problem and has tried other cures is vulnerable. He may grab at any implied or direct promise for help that comes along, and especially from a medical doctor. This is the very predicament in which many Christians find themselves.

Few people realize that medical hypnosis is *any* hypnosis used for medical purposes. Medical doctors use both hypnotic regression and deep hypnosis. At what point in hypnotic regression and at what depth in hypnosis should a Christian discontinue hypnotic treatment? Some medical doctors use a medical hypnosis which encourages a type of dissociation. The individual becomes an observer of his own body and helps in diagnosis and treatment. They have "the hypnotized patient mentally 'go into' the appropriate area of the body to do repairs, to help medicine be effective or to see the healing process at work."[7] Would this type of medical hypnosis be acceptable to a Christian?

The following is a description of Jack Schwartz, who has conducted experiments at the Menninger Foundation using a visualization technique (equivalent to hypnosis) to heal a cut hand:

> First, he instructs, use your mind to see yourself sitting there. Look at your hand (in your mind). Separate the hand from the body, and let it move away from you, growing larger and larger.
>
> Then, in your mind, rise and walk toward it. Halfway there, look back at your body in the chair. Tell it to do a task, like crossing its legs. If it complies, face the hand. Move toward it, entering it through a door. Visualize yourself inside, looking at the cut. See yourself repairing the cut with glue or tape. Continue working—visually—until the cut is repaired.

Come out, and walk back to your body. When
you look at the large mind-body hand off in the
distance, you see it is healed. It moves toward you
and slips back into place, ending the visualization.
Thank your body, and picture it as a whole and
full of joy.[8]

We raise the following questions about the use of
hypnosis by a medical doctor: How can one tell the long-
range spiritual effect of even a well-meaning medical
doctor's use of hypnosis on a Christian patient? Would
an M.D. with an anti-Christian or occult bias in any
way affect a Christian through trance treatment? How
about the use of a medical hypnotherapist who belongs
to the Satanist church? What about an M.D.
hypnotherapist who uses past or future lives therapy
as a means of mental-emotional or physical relief?
These and other questions need to be answered before
subjecting oneself to such treatment, even in the hands
of a medical doctor or psychologist.

We wrote to Professor Ernest Hilgard, one of the
most-respected, leading authorities on hypnosis, at
Stanford University and asked two questions in our
quest for information:

1. Have any follow-up studies been done five years
   or more after hypnosis has been used to relieve
   pain, change behavior, etc.? We are particularly
   interested in finding out if the results are long
   lasting.

2. What is the difference between hypnosis as used
   by a trained practitioner and that used by
   shamans or witch doctors?[9]

Hilgard's reply to the first question was:

> Long term studies are scarce, but the results of
> hypnotic treatment are commonly made more per-
> manent through the teaching of self-hypnosis.[10]

However, long term studies of those using self-
hypnosis are also scarce. Therefore we have little to no
valid information about the long term effects on the
individual as the result of hypnosis. We particularly
have no information we could find on the long term
spiritual effect on Christians who submit themselves
to this treatment.

In reply to the second question, Hilgard wrote:

> Trained practitioners know a great deal about
> contemporary psychotherapy and hypnosis is
> merely adjuvant. In this they differ from those
> whose practices are essentially magical.[11]

In short, the difference between a shaman and a
trained practitioner of hypnosis is that the trained
practitioner will use hypnosis with psychotherapy.
Notice that Hilgard does not distinguish the hypnosis
used by the hypnotherapist from that of the shaman
except that the hypnotherapist uses hypnosis with
psychotherapy.

Hypno-Psycho-Religious Synthesis

Joseph Palotta, a professing Christian who is also a
psychiatrist and hypnotherapist, combines the worst
of two evils into a practice that he calls "hypnoanalysis." His system is an amalgamation of hypnosis and
the Freudian psychosexual states of development. His

book *The Robot Psychiatrist* is filled with unproven Freudian concepts, such as subconscious determinants, abreaction and the supposed determinism of early life experiences. He says that his book contains "extremely rapid systems of treatment for emotional disorders." He promises, "These methods bring about definite therapeutic change of the underlying emotional problem."[12]

Palotta is completely sold on the Oedipus complex. He, like Freud, claims that this is "a universal experience in the emotional development of every person."[13] The Oedipus Complex states that every child is filled with a desire for incest and homicide, every child desires sexual intercourse with the parent of the opposite sex, every child wants the like-sex parent to die, and every child is confronted with castration anxiety. Palotta says:

> The universal conclusion that little boys and little girls make is that somehow the little girls have lost their penises and have nothing.[14]

He goes on to describe how "little girls feel that they have been castrated, that their penises have somehow been cut off" and that little boys "fear that they will lose their penises." He says, "The little girls develop what is termed penis envy." According to Freud, every girl is merely a mutilated male who resolves her castration anxiety by wishing for the male sex organ. As Freud's theories are unveiled, we see lust, incest, castration anxiety, and for a woman penis envy. Freud was convinced that all of these are psychologically determined by age five or six. Can you think of a more macabre, twisted and demonic explanation for human problems?

The Oedipus Complex is based on the Greek play *Oedipus Rex* by Sophocles. Thomas Szasz, a psychiatrist who is well trained in Freudian ideas and well aware of their origins, says, "By dint of his rhetorical skill and persistence, Freud managed to transform an Athenian myth into an Austrian madness." He calls this "Freud's transformation of the saga of Oedipus from legend to lunacy."[15] So, the first evil is Freudian psychology at its worst, and the second evil is the use of hypnosis.

Palotta attempts to support his system of hypnosis and psychoanalysis through describing certain individual cases, which he claims "are typical of experiences with hypnoanalysis in the practice of Christian psychiatry."[16] Palotta is educated enough to know that using his cases to prove success are invalid because there are no third party experts checking him out. Nevertheless he uses these cases to support his hypnoanalytic practice. Palotta describes a case of a 25-year-old mother who experienced anxiety and fear. Palotta says:

> Analysis of her fear under hypnosis revealed that at age four she witnessed her father in a drunken rage, fighting with her mother, and then coming toward the patient with a knife in his hand. Her next memory was fainting, then getting out of bed, kneeling, and praying to God to take her then, to remove her from that awful environment. When God didn't take her, she decided, "I hate God."
>
> She was then re-educated under hypnosis to correct the error that she had to die to be okay.[17]

Palotta claims to have helped this woman through hypnosis and psychoanalysis because "it provided the insight necessary for her to begin a course of emotional and spiritual healing." Personal, unsubstantiated claims by Palotta and others with no means of checking and no long term follow up tell us nothing of value about his system. We have numerous claims by a variety of hypnotherapists who say they have cured such illnesses as:

1. Migraine headaches.
2. Obsessive eating and obesity.
3. Bulemia.
4. Stuttering.
5. Parkinson's syndrome.
6. Chronic stiff neck.
7. Chronic jaw pain.
8. Arthritis.[18]

One hypnotherapist claims to have enlarged women's breasts and even to have dissolved a kidney stone.[19] Should we accept all these unverified cases by these hypnotherapists without proof?

Palotta promises much from his hypno-psycho-analytical merger. However, recent writings from both in and out of the psychiatric profession indicate that the Freudian concepts are in question because of their tainted origins and because their tarnished history predicts a tenuous future for them. The major Freudian ideas have neither stood the test of time nor withstood the scrutiny of research. Palotta provides a prime example of one who has combined the fallacies of Freud with the hypocrisy of hypnosis. He attempts to synthesize his theories and to synchronize them with Scripture, but it is a false alchemy.

Hypnosis and the Occult in Medicine

Szasz laments the fact that "hypnosis enjoys periodic revivals as a 'medical treatment.'"[20] We are presently in such a revival and some individuals in the church have already opened wide the door to "medical" hypnotherapy. However, medical doctors also prescribe holistic health practices such as meditation, visual imagery, and biofeedback. Systems or techniques used by medical doctors are not automatically medical or scientific, despite their labels. *Brain/Mind* bulletin describes a new approach to improving personal performance called *sophrology:*

> Sophrology combines exercises in relaxation, breathing, body-awareness, visualization, self-hypnosis and autogenics (control of automatic body functions). The exercises aim to enhance attention, perception, concentration, precision of movement, efficiency and control of posture.

This report says that sophrology is a combining of principles "of Eastern and Western mind and body disciplines." There are now over 5,000 physicians who have been trained in this Eastern-Western approach which includes "Raja yoga, Zen, and Tibetan practices."[21] Just because this approach is being used by medical doctors should not assure us that it is either scientific or acceptable to the Christian in need of help.

In their book *Psychic Healing,* John Weldon and Zola Levitt observe, "The current trend is moving toward more professionals (scientists, physicians, psychologists, etc.) and lay health professionals seeking to develop occult abilities."[22] They say:

> An increasing number of practitioners in the healing profession (M.D.'s nurses, chiropractors, etc.) are being swayed by psychic philosophies and practices, largely due to the influence of parapsychology, psychic healing, and the holistic health movements.

They warn:

> Patients can no longer afford the luxury of failing to determine the spiritual status of those who treat them. Failure to ascertain that may be more costly than a yearly medical bill. Practices that look entirely innocent . . . can become the means of occult bondage.[23]

The integration of Eastern mystical and Eastern medical traditions into Western medicine requires great discernment as to what is medical and what is mystical. Medical doctor Arthur Deikman says, "I now regard mysticism as a type of science. . . . A mystic's motive for behaving virtuously differs sharply from that of a religious devotee. . . . This distinction shows mysticism to be a psychological science rather than a belief system."[24]

Transcendental Meditation, also known as TM, is a combination of religion and psychotherapy. Many medical doctors now use TM for healing numerous psychological and physical problems. TM is sometimes referred to as the "Science of Creative Intelligence." But TM is *not* medicine and it is *not* science. According to a judge in New Jersey, it is a religion and cannot be taught in public schools because of the guaranteed separation of church and state.[25]

The label of *science* is misapplied to all of the above and to hypnotism as well. In addition to sophrology, yoga, and TM, some therapists use astrology, the I Ching, Tantra, Tarot, alchemy and Actualism, all of which are occult practices.[26] This confusion of science with the occult is very evident in hypnotism.

Compounding the word *hypnosis* with the word *therapy* does not lift the practice from the occult to the scientific, nor is hypnotherapy any more dignified than hypnosis as practiced by witchdoctors. The white coat may be a more respectable uniform than feathers and face paint, but the basics are the same. Hypnosis is hypnosis whether it is called medical hypnosis, hypnotherapy, autosuggestion, or anything else. Hypnosis in the hands of a medical doctor is as scientific as a dowsing rod in the hands of a civil engineer.

Newsweek magazine reports on hypnosis in hospital settings:

> At Walter Reed and other hospitals, hypnosis has been used as the principle or only anesthetic for such procedures as Caesarean sections, and the literature documents gallbladder and prostate surgery, appendectomies, thyroidectomies, minor amputations and skin grafts also done under hypnosis.[27]

The Dallas Morning News reported on the fragmentation theory, which is supposedly behind why hypnosis works in such situations:

The fragmentation theory is supported by studies of highly hypnosis-susceptible individuals. When subjected to pain during a trance, they often have what is known as a "hidden observer" that metaphorically records the amount of pain experienced but does not let the pain come to consciousness. The hidden observer was discovered in the 1970s when subjects were asked to have the "part" of themselves that experienced the pain write down how much pain they experienced through a number scale while simultaneously having the other part verbally tell the hypnotist what they felt. Many subjects wrote that they experienced a high degree of pain at some level while telling the hypnotist they felt nothing.[28]

Ernest R. Hilgard explains how the fragmentation theory works in simpler terms. He says, "Some hidden part of the mind registers things that are going on, while another part is occupied with something else and is unaware of what's going on." He says it is as if "part of you is on this stage and part of you is out in the wings watching."[29]

What is the long term effect of this dichotomy of the person explained by the fragmentation theory? Since the "hidden observer" is a more widespread phenomena than just cases of hypnosis associated with pain, what effect might this type of dissociation have on the individual's personality? We could find no research to address these questions.

Open Door of Pragmatism

Some people use pragmatism to support the practice of hypnotism. They say that since it works it must be good. The pain may disappear, sleep may be attained, and sex life may improve. Who can criticize such a procedure? However, does the end justify the means? Many witchdoctors and shamans have higher cure rates than hypnotherapists. Results should not be the evidence for promoting and utilizing hypnotism.

Immediate positive results from hypnotism should especially be dismissed as evidence for validity of the practice, since many who gain initial victory over problems later suffer defeat. The pain which was "cured" may return, the sleep turns again into sleeplessness, and the temporarily improved sex life deteriorates. In spite of numerous claims and testimonials, research has not demonstrated that hypnosis is any more effective for chronic pain than a placebo. After examining the research, two researchers confess:

> Despite a vast amount of excellent research on the effects of hypnosis on experimentally induced pain, there is virtually no reliable evidence from controlled clinical studies to show that it is effective for any form of chronic pain.[30]

Besides this possibility of the quick cure, short-term change with later failure, there is the possibility of symptom substitution. For example, those who are relieved of migraine headaches through hypnosis may end up with ulcers. A study conducted at the famous Diamond Headache Clinic in Chicago revealed the strong possibility of symptom substitution. They found that of those migraine patients who had learned to control headaches through biofeedback, "two-thirds reported the development of new psychosomatic symptoms within five years."[31]

If indeed hypnosis may result in occult healing, there are potential serious consequences to consider. Weldon and Levitt say, "We would expect that most if not all of those who are occultly healed are likely to suffer either psychologically or spiritually in some way."[32] Kurt Koch, in his book *Demonology: Past and Present,* says that in occult forms of healing:

> The original organic illness is shifted higher into the psychical realm, with the result that while the physical illness disappears, new disorders appear in the mental and emotional life of the person concerned, disorders which are in fact far more difficult to treat and cure. Magical healings are therefore not really healings at all, but merely transferences from the organic to the psychical level.[33]

Koch believes that the power behind occult healing is *demonic,* that such healing serves as an *impediment* to a person's spiritual life, and that the damage is *immense.* Weldon and Levitt also point out that occult practices do provide healing but that the cure is often worse than the original illness. They say:

> In conclusion, psychic healing is not a part of the natural or latent capacities of man. It is a distinctly supernatural, spiritistic power and carries grave consequences both for those who practice it and for those healed by it. Those who practice it may have no indication that spirit entities are the real source of their power, but that does not reduce their own responsibility for the spiritual and psycho-logical destruction of those they heal. There is

always a high price to pay when contacting forces alien to God.[34]

Koch says:

> Although certain Christian workers believe that some types of healing mesmerism [a form of hypnotism] are dependent on neutral rather than mediumistic powers, I would say that I have personally hardly ever come across a neutral form. Many years of experience in this field have shown me that even in the case of Christian mesmerisers the basic mediumship has always come to the surface in the end.[35]

In his book *Occult ABC* Koch says:

> We must distinguish between the hypnosis used by doctors for diagnosis and treatment and magically based hypnosis, which is clearly occult in character. But I must not neglect to add, that I reject even the kind of hypnosis used by doctors.[36]

A fact rarely mentioned by hypnotists is that whatever physical healing is accomplished with hypnosis can also be accomplished without it. The *Modern Synopsis of Comprehensive Textbook of Psychiatry / II* states, "Everything done in psychotherapy with hypnosis can also be done without hypnosis."[37] We believe that it is not only unnecessary to use hypnosis but potentially dangerous. Even though hypnosis may currently be used by medical doctors, it originated from and is still practiced by witch doctors. Even medical hypnosis practiced by a Christian may be a disguised doorway and subtle enticement into the demonic realm. It may not be as obvious an entree to evil as occult hypnosis, and therefore it could be even more dangerous for an unsuspecting Christian who would otherwise avoid the occult.

Are people in the church being enticed to enter the twilight zone of the occult because hypnosis is now called "science" and "medicine"? Let those who call the occult "science" tell us what the difference is between medical and occultic hypnosis. And let those Christians who call it "scientific" explain why they also recommend that it be performed **only** by a Christian. If hypnosis is science indeed, why the added requirement of Christianity for the practitioner? There is a scarcity of adequate long-term studies of those who have been hypnotized. And there have been none which have examined the effect on the individual's resulting faith or interest in the occult.

10

The Bible and Hypnosis

Hypnosis has been among the dark arts throughout ancient history until the present. In his book on the history of hypnosis, Maurice Tinterow says, "Probably the early soothsayers and oracles relied largely on the hypnotic state."[1] The Bible does not treat occult practices as harmless superstitions; neither does it deny the authenticity or helpful effects of such practices. However, there are strong warnings against all that is associated with the occult. God desires His people to come to Him with their needs rather than turn to occult practitioners.

The Bible strongly speaks out against having anything to do with those who involve themselves in the occult because of the demonic power, influence, and control. Occult activities were practiced by the nations surrounding Israel during the time of Moses. Therefore God explicitly warned His people against them:

> Ye shall not eat any thing with the blood: neither
> shall ye use enchantment, nor observe times. . . .
> Regard not them that have familiar spirits, neither
> seek after wizards, to be defiled by them: I am the
> Lord your God (Lev. 19:26, 31).

> There shall not be found among you any one that
> maketh his son or his daughter to pass through
> the fire, or that useth divination, or an observer of
> times, or an enchanter, or a witch, or a charmer, or
> a consulter with familiar spirits, or a wizard, or a
> necromancer. For all that do these things are an
> abomination unto the Lord: and because of these
> abominations the Lord thy God doth drive them
> out from before thee (Deut. 18:10-12).

Because of the apparent occult nature of hypnosis
(which is more obvious in the deeper stages) and
because hypnosis is practiced by many who involve
themselves in other areas of the occult, Christians
would be wise to avoid hypnosis even for medical
purposes.

The words from the Old Testament which are trans-
lated *charmers* and *enchanters* seem to indicate the
same kinds of persons whom we now call
hypnotherapists. Dave Hunt, author of *The Cult Explosion*[2] and *Occult Invasion*[3] and researcher in the
area of the occult as well as the cults, says:

> From the Biblical standpoint, I believe that in such
> places as Deuteronomy 18, when it speaks of
> "charmers" and "enchanters," the practice involved
> anciently was exactly what has recently become
> acceptable in medicine and psychiatry as hypno-

sis. I believe this both from the ancient usage of this word and from occult traditions.[4]

A Watchman Fellowship "Profile" says the following:

It is difficult to know if "charming" is a direct reference to hypnosis as the evidence is somewhat circumstantial. The Bible, however, is replete with clear admonitions against involvement with the occult (Leviticus 19:26; 2 Kings 21:6; Isaiah 47:9-13; Acts 8:9-11). This would prohibit any Christian association in those aspects of hypnosis that directly relate to the occult (spiritualism, channeling, past-life regression, divination, etc.).

There is general agreement that hypnotized individuals are somewhat vulnerable to uncritically accepting as true any suggestion given by the hypnotist. This factor alone creates the potential for misuse and deception. Some Christian researchers go a step further warning that it is possible for hypnotized subjects to be influenced by voices other than that of the hypnotist. They believe that in a trance state one is more susceptible to demonic oppression or even possession— especially if the subject has a history of occult experimentation .

Hypnosis can be indirectly linked to biblical admonitions against "charming." It is historically linked to pagan and occult practices. Even proponents warn of the potential for misuse or unethical application. These factors coupled with the absence of a provable neutral, non-religious theory

of hypnosis make hypnosis a potentially dangerous practice not recommended for Christians.[5]

Just because hypnosis has surfaced in medicine does
not mean that it is different from the ancient practices of charmers and enchanters or from those which
have been used more recently by witchdoctors and
occult hypnotists. John Weldon and Zola Levitt say that
even "a strictly scientific approach toward occult
phenomena is insufficient protection against
demonism. The judgment of God does not distinguish
between scientific and nonscientific involvement with
powers alien to Him."[6]

In various sections of Scripture, occult practices are
listed side by side, because although one activity may
differ from the next, the power source and the revealer
of "hidden knowledge" is the same: Satan. Enchanters, sorcerers, wizards, charmers, consulters of familiar spirits, necromancers, soothsayers, and observers
of times (astrologers) are grouped together as those to
avoid. See Lev. 19:26, 31, and 20:6, 27; Deut. 18:9-14; 2
Kings 21:6; 2 Chron. 33:6; Isa. 47:9-13; Jer. 27:9. A
singular word for those practicing the occult is used in
the New Testament: *sorcerer.*

All forms of the occult turn a person away from God
to self and to those spirits in opposition to God. That is
why God compares using sorcery to "playing the harlot."

And the soul that turneth after such as have
familiar spirits, and after wizards, to go a whor-
ing after them, I will even set my face against that
soul, and will cut him off from among his people
(Lev. 20:6).

Almighty God saw these practices as replacing relationship with himself. He saw them as false religions with false religious experiences.

As noted earlier, many who support hypnosis say that religion uses hypnosis and that Christian experiences involving prayer, meditation, confession, devotion, and worship are actually forms of self-hypnosis. Perhaps the reasons why hypnotists see these similarities is that hypnosis generates Satan's counterfeits of true religious exercise. If indeed hypnosis involves any form of faith and worship not directed toward the God of the Bible, any person who subjects himself to hypnotism may be playing the harlot in the spiritual realm.

In hypnotism faith is shifted to the hypnotist and to the practice of hypnotism. In this state of increased suggestibility, the individual opens his mind to suggestions which might be otherwise rejected. Obedience and even an eagerness to please the hypnotist occur in many instances. The hypnotist takes the place of priest or God and holds that place throughout the trance until he either releases the subject or the subject meets a "higher guide" within the trance. Some persons remain locked into this relationship even after the trance through post-hypnotic suggestion.

Psychology Today published an article titled "Hypnosis may be hazardous," which says:

A teenage girl with no history of psychological problems was hypnotized on stage as part of a show. Soon after leaving with her friends, she apparently reentered the trance. No one could rouse her. She had to be hospitalized and fed intravenously, and took months to recover.

While such life-threatening emergencies stem-
ming from the use of hypnosis are rare, reports of
a wide range of unwanted aftereffects are on the
rise, according to psychologist Frank MacHovec,
who has been studying and treating hypnosis
casualties for 16 years. He estimates that 1 in 10
people who have been hypnotized will experience
some difficulties as a direct result.[7]

MacHovec reveals a variety of ways in which
hypnosis has been detrimental to individuals. However, hypnosis is not only personally dangerous to
people; it is spiritually dangerous. An individual may
become vulnerable to occult powers when he is in a
state of heightened suggestion and distorted reality.

Many people do not realize their vulnerability to
hypnosis when it is used in other contexts. For instance,
in describing New Age mysticism used in training sessions for business, Richard Watring says:

Most of the techniques described are either
tantamount to a hypnotic induction or their use
renders the individual more highly suggestible to
hypnotic induction. Most people know what
hypnosis is, but very few people know that the use
of affirmation, suggestology, neurolinguistic
programming, some forms of guided imagery, est
and est-type human potential seminars employ
some of the same dynamics as hypnosis.[8]

The Spiritual Counterfeits Project has revealed how
New Age thinking is dangerous to Christians. They
say:

New Age thinking has been expressed in the holistic health movement in two ways. One expression strongly emphasizes consciousness-altering techniques (such as Eastern forms of meditation, visualization, and even out-of-body experiences). Many spokespeople teach that healing occurs spontaneously when one has an experience of oneness with the universe through one of those processes.

A second, more diversified, expression comes from the belief that a universal "life energy"— which is usually considered identical to what religions call God—flows through all objects, both living and inanimate.[9]

Notice how close this description matches experiences in the hypnotic state. "Visualization," "out-of-body experiences," and "an experience of oneness with the universe" all occur in hypnosis. And, the "universal 'life energy'" is similar to Mesmer's idea of "an invisible fluid," which he called "animal magnetism" and which he considered to be an energy existing throughout nature. Many of the New Age ingredients are in hypnosis; all the warning signs are there.

Why Do Christians Use Hypnosis?

Since most hypnosis practitioners know that hypnosis is an occult practice, why do professing Christians use it? These professing Christian practitioners give various reasons and justifications. We will look at three examples. The first is from a Christian hypnotherapist who wrote to us and said:

> For 10 years I used hypnosis on thousands of
> people dozens of times and failed to find it to be
> satanic mind control, etc. Of course the occult use
> hypnosis. They also use sex, money, cars, food, and
> the Bible. All hypnosis is is a heightened state of
> relaxation and suggestibility and an altered state
> of consciousness.[10]

This sounds like the logical fallacy of false analogy.
The following is a textbook description of *false analogy*.

> To recognize the fallacy of false analogy, look for
> an argument that draws a conclusion about one
> thing, event, or practice on the basis of its anal-
> ogy or resemblance to others. The fallacy occurs
> when the analogy or resemblance is not sufficient
> to warrant the conclusion, as when, for example,
> the resemblance is not relevant to the possession
> of the inferred feature or there are relevant
> dissimilarities.[11]

The occult and Christian use of "sex, money, cars,
food, and the Bible" is in no way equivalent to both
groups using hypnosis. Also, hypnosis originated from
the occult and is an occult activity itself, which is not
true of "sex, money, cars, food, and the Bible."

The second example comes from H. Newton Maloney,
a professor at Fuller Seminary. Maloney also uses the
logical fallacy of false analogy to justify his use of
hypnosis:

> The ideal Christian response to God has consis-
> tently been pictured as single minded devotion in

which one puts aside the distractions of the world. If hypnotists help persons achieve this skill they are well within the spectrum of what true life is all about. If one assumes that the optimal state of mind would be that in which persons know what they wanted and pursued it without distraction, then the hypnotic state would be the norm rather than the waking state in which persons either deny their true selves or are unable to focus their attention because of many distractions.[12]

Maloney uses similarities in language to justify using an occult activity to worship or experience devotion to God.

The third example is that of medical doctor George Newbold, who says:

It is my belief that in a trance-state the mind becomes more susceptible to spiritual influences— again for good or ill. If this is so, then any medium may lay himself or herself open to Satanic attack by evil spirits. If Satan can utilize the trance in this way we also have biblical evidence that God does so as well.

In the Old Testament there are many examples of how the Lord revealed Himself to the prophets through visions. Balaam, for instance, "saw the vision of the Almighty, falling into a trance, but having his eyes open" (Num. 24:4). Similarly, in the New Testament both Peter and Paul recount how they fell into a trance while praying (Acts 11:5 and 22:17).[13]

Newbold equates hypnosis, an occult activity, with a biblical vision and concludes that both Satan and God can use the trance. One does not need a logic book to figure out what's wrong with his thinking. Newbold admits:

> The fear that hypnosis is somehow inseparable from the practice of spiritualism and the occult needs to be taken seriously. The reason for this lies in the occurrence of so-called "paranormal" phenomena during the state of trance which bears a close resemblance to hypnosis.
>
> If we exclude cases of fraud, nearly all spiritualistic seances are conducted with a medium in the peculiar psychological condition known as a "trance" in which the participant is in a state of altered consciousness and may appear to be acting as an automaton during somnambulistic episodes.[14]

Newbold fails to explain how such paranormal experiences or demonic influence during hypnosis can be avoided in medical hypnosis. Also, because of the scarcity of long-term studies and the fact that many individuals use self hypnosis with unexamined results, no one really knows what happens to the faith and belief systems of Christians who submit themselves to hypnosis.

Demonic influence may not be clearly apparent in many instances of hypnosis, but the mind has been tampered with in discerning truth. There may indeed be an opening or influence into other areas of the occult and areas of deception. One of Jesus' warnings about the last days was spiritual deception. Satan is the master deceiver and if a person has opened his mind to deception through hypnosis, he may be more vulnerable to spiritual deception.

Hypnosis has been an integral part of the occult. Therefore a Christian should not allow himself to be hypnotized for any reason. The promises of help through hypnosis are very similar to the promises of help through other occultic healers. The Christian has another spiritual means of help: the Lord God Himself!

11

Hypnosis in Unexpected Places

While the focus of this book is specifically hypnosis, the characteristics underlying trance states (altered states of consciousness) exist elsewhere. Thus while the settings and situations will not always produce a trance state, the danger is nonetheless there.

Regressive Therapy and Inner Healing

Therapists who attempt to help clients remember events and feelings from their childhood often use hypnotic techniques that actually move clients into a trance state. They may deny using hypnosis, but guided imagery and other techniques used in leading a person back into the past are hypnotic induction devices. As quoted earlier, Michael Yapko, author of *Trancework*, says:

Many times therapists aren't even aware that they're doing hypnosis. They're doing what they call guided imagery or guided meditation, which are all very mainstream hypnotic techniques.[1]

The suggestions, the emotions, and the focus on feelings in the past rarely produce true memories. In various forms of regressive therapy the therapist attempts to convince the client that present problems are from past hurtful events and then proceeds to help the client remember and re-experience hurtful events in the past. However, rather than positive change, many false memories are produced.

Some writers, such as Campbell Perry, indicate that **such techniques as the eliciting of memories, relaxation, and regression work are often disguised forms of hypnosis**. In introducing his paper on controversies regarding the False Memory Syndrome (FMS), Perry describes some of the procedures that:

> . . . appear to be strongly linked with the development of a subjectively convincing memory that a person (usually a woman) was sexually abused during childhood by (usually) her father, that the putative memory has been repressed, only to seemingly resurface during the course of "recovered memory" therapy. Special emphasis is placed upon the role of "disguised" hypnosis in eliciting such memories—that is, upon procedures that are characterized by such terms as guided imagery, "relaxation," dream analysis, regression work and sodium amytal represented as "truth serum." All of these appear to tap into the mechanisms thought to underly the experience of hypnosis.[2]

The leading questions, direct guidance, and voice intonation are enough to serve as an induction into the trance state for many individuals. Mark Pendergrast says:

> The "guided imagery" exercises that trauma therapists employ to gain access to buried memories can be enormously convincing, whether we choose to call the process hypnosis or not. When someone is relaxed, willing to suspend critical judgment, engage in fantasy, and place ultimate faith in an authority figure using ritualistic methods, deceptive scenes from the past can easily be induced.[3]

Various forms of regressive psychotherapy and inner healing with the use of visualization, guided imagery, powerful suggestion, and intense concentration can very easily result in inducing a hypnotic state in which the person experiences so-called memories as if they are presently occurring. There are numerous problems with inner healing, some of which we discuss in our book *TheoPhostic Counseling: Divine Revelation or PsychoHeresy*? Many of the techniques used to rouse the imagination and intensify the feelings encourage the hypnotic state through intense suggestion. Regressive therapy and inner healing have the same possibilities and dangers as discussed in the previous chapters on hypnosis.

Those who practice and promote regressive therapy and inner healing believe that the source of problems and therefore the necessary location of healing is within the unconscious or subconscious. Many inner healers, following the influence of Agnes Sanford, attempt to bring Jesus into the person's unconscious for healing. In her book *The Healing Gifts of the Spirit*, Sanford says, "The Lord will walk back with you into the memories of the past so they will be healed."[4]

Medical doctor Jane Gumprecht, in her book *Abusing Memory: The Healing Theology of Agnes Sanford*, outlines the seven steps of Sanford's method, which could easily lead a person into an altered state of consciousness through emptying the mind, following the voice of the inner healer, and visualizing according to suggestion:

> 1. *Jesus enters the collective unconscious to redeem memories.* She explained that healing of memories is redemption for which Jesus entered into the "collective unconscious"; humans are bound by time so Jesus is our "Time Traveler"; "the Lord will walk back with you into the memories of the past so that they will be healed."
>
> 2. *Know the patient's childhood.* She inquired about their childhood. . . .
>
> 3. *Wait for them to get over fears and embarrassments.* Knowing that they were "holding something back out of fear or embarrassment," she waited for the rest to come forth.
>
> 4. *Clear the mind.* She had the patient relax, meditate (empty the mind) as she did with her prayer of faith. She laid hands on them to "transfer the love of Christ into them."
>
> 5. *See Jesus interacting with their inner child.* She prayed and had the patient use their creative imagination to visualize Jesus taking them back through time to the scene during their childhood

when they were hurt and felt unloved, relive the emotions involved.

6. *Pray for healing, even for times before birth.* She prayed for the Lord to "go back through all the rooms of this memory-house . . . see if there be any dirty and broken things . . . take them completely away . . . go back even to the nursery in this memory house . . . back to the hour of birth . . . even before birth if the soul was shadowed by this human life and was darkened by the fears and sorrows of the human parents."

7. *See yourself as God meant you to be.* "Power of visioning; in the healing of memories one must firmly hold in the imagination the picture of this person as God meant him to be, seeing through the human aberrations and perversions . . . and turn in the imagination the dark and awful shadows of his nature into shining virtues and sources of power. This is redemption."[5]

Gumprecht further reveals Sanford's use of double-bind and suggestion:

Not only did [Sanford] ask leading questions of those who admit to an unhappy childhood; she planted the seed of suggestion and doubt in the mind of those who had a happy childhood. I have found that those who have written books on *Healing of Memories* (David Seamands) and *Transformation of the Inner Man* (John and Paula Sandford) do the same thing—working hard through suggestion until the patient finally dredged up some hurt from his past.[6]

While undergoing this practice called inner healing, some may possibly avoid moving into a hypnotic trance. Others, especially those who are most vulnerable to hypnotic suggestion, will easily drift into a trance.

Large Group Awareness Training

The Forum (formerly est), Life Spring, and Momentus are the names of some of the more well-known large-group training seminars that promise life-transforming results. Using many of the ideas and techniques of the encounter movement, such group sessions attempt to alter participants' present way of thinking (mind set, world view, personal faith, etc.) through intense personal and group experiences. Some have marathon meetings that last numerous hours and take advantage of fatigue working together with much repetition, group pressure and various psychological techniques, some of which attack personal belief systems and cause mental confusion.

The confusion technique, which is also a hypnotic device, may be used to disorient the subject to make him more responsive to cues. Michael Yapko says:

> In the confusion technique, you give a person more information than they could possibly keep up with, you get them to question everything, you make them feel uncertain as a way of building up their motivation to attain certainty.[7]

While hypnosis may not be intended or admitted in such large group training sessions, the possibility is very strong for participants to experience hypnotic suggestion, dissociation, and impaired personal judgment.

Music

Music, including Christian music, comes in a variety of forms and beats. In his book *The Way of the Shaman*, Michael Harner, who is a shaman, describes the Shamanic State of Consciousness (SSC). He also delineates the shamanic journey of a shaman in a SSC. He explains how a companion can assist the shaman in his SSC journey by providing specific drum beats. He says:

> Now instruct your companion to start beating the drum in a strong, monotonous, unvarying, and rapid beat. There should be no contrast in intensity of the drum beats or in the intervals between them. A drumming tempo of about 205 to 220 beats per minute is usually effective for this journey.[8]

We are not saying that such a shamanic beat will transport one into a SSC and prepare the individual for a shamanic journey, but it certainly can. Neither are we saying that Christian music will transport one into a trance, but it may with certain susceptible people.

Repetitive sounds and words can also induce an altered state of consciousness. Hindus, for instance, use the concept of OM in working spiritually with consciousness. In his book *The Secret Power of Music*, David Tame says:

> In this spiritual endeavour the concept of OM, as the earthly sound which mirrors the Sound of the One Tone, is paramount. Intoning the OM, in

combination with certain mental and spiritual disciplines, is of prime importance in raja yoga. In
some meditation techniques the OM is not actually uttered at all, but simply imagined with the
inner ear, consequently attuning the soul directly
with the Soundless Sound.[9]

Tame further describes how music is used to assist
in bringing the mind to a "point of concentration":

Music even aids, it is believed, in the raising of
the "vibration" or spiritual frequency of the body
itself, beginning the process of the transformation
of matter into spirit, and consequently returning
matter to its original state. Thus, as all is OM, the
OM as music calls to the OM as manifested in the
soul of man, to draw it back to the Source of the
OM itself.[10]

This certainly sounds familiar to descriptions of deep
hypnosis.

Most music will not elicit an altered state of
consciousness. However, one should be aware that
rhythm and tone can indeed be used to induce a trance.

Church Services

In addition to the music, a pastor or church leader
may inadvertently and naively use hypnotic inductive
techniques as he sets the mood, prays, or speaks. Those
who may be especially susceptible to these hypnotic
devices may indeed go into a trance, especially in healing services in which people are led into a kind of mystical expectation, in which thinking is set aside and a
mystical, waiting attitude is encouraged. A variety of

factors work together to produce this possibility: type of music, a leader's prestige or charisma, expectations for healing or miracles, peer pressure, suggestions made by the leader and the suggestibility of the audience. While each of these may work alone to lead persons into a trance state, collectively they almost guarantee an altered state of consciousness for some who are in attendance.

While some of the activity in the so-called revivals where people swoon to the floor, jerk around, and bark like dogs may be due to intentional participation, much may be due to hypnosis. We do NOT agree with the following statement, which was quoted earlier:

> Hypnotic trance occurs regularly in all Christian congregations. Those who most condemn it as diabolical are the very ones who tend to induce hypnotic trance most often—unaware that they are doing so.[11]

However, we are concerned about Christian meetings that encourage mindless emotionality and spiritual activities that could result in hypnotic trance induced behavior.

We are also concerned when the evangelist or preacher becomes the focus of attention in the same way as the hypnotist. There's a strong possibility of trance induction having taken place when people fall over backwards when touched by certain healers. Whenever repetition to the point of hypnotic actions or words or songs is used, a trance state may be induced. Techniques appealing to emotion, imagination, and visualization over the intellect and active volition are often hypnotic induction devices. Any use of hypnotic techniques in worship is potentially dangerous to the faith of those in attendance.

Prayer and Meditation

Certain forms of prayer and meditation in which the individual is passive in a similar way as in the above description can lead to hypnotic trance. As mentioned earlier, yoga and similar forms of meditation are means of being hypnotized. Transcendental Meditation with its repetition of a single word or phrase can result in an altered state of consciousness, as in the repetition of OM.

One article reporting on brain electrical activity during prayer and during Transcendental Meditation states:

> It would appear that the individual's state of consciousness during prayer is quite different from that reported to occur during Transcendental Meditation.[12]

In contrast to meditation, the prayers recorded in Scripture are active. The mind is active as in conversation. Prayer is indeed conversation in which the person prays according to his knowledge of God, which he has learned through God's part of the conversation: the Bible, the living Word of God. There is active dialog in biblical prayer in that as a person prays, the Holy Spirit may bring to mind truths and promises from God's Word. However, when a person attempts to move into a mystical, passive mental state in prayer, he may indeed move into a hypnotic trance. The closer he stays to the Word of God in prayer and the less he aims for a feeling state, the more biblical the prayer and the less the possibility for moving into a hypnotic trance.

Medical Offices

While not all biofeedback activities will induce a trance state, many can. The following are common self-talk sentences used in one biofeedback activity:

> My whole body feels relaxed and my mind is quiet.
> I release my attention from the outside world.
> I feel serene and still.
> I can gently visualize, imagine and experience myself as relaxed and still.
> I feel inward quietness.
> I am at peace.

This is similar to medical doctor Herbert Benson's Relaxation Response, which has been described as:

> . . . the ability of the body to enter into a scientifically defined state characterized by an overall reduction of the speed of the body's metabolism, lowered blood pressure, decreased rate of breathing, lowered heart rate, and more prominent, slower brain waves.[13]

Benson says:

> There are several basic steps required to elicit the Relaxation Response.
> Step 1: Pick a focus word or short phrase that's firmly rooted in your personal belief system. For example, a Christian person might choose the opening words of Psalm 23, "The

Lord is my shepherd"; a Jewish person, "Sha-
lom"; a nonreligious individual a neutral
word like "one" or "peace."

Step 2: Sit quietly in a comfortable position.

Step 3: Close your eyes.

Step 4: Relax your muscles.

Step 5: Breathe slowly and naturally, and as
you do, repeat your focus word or phrase as
you exhale.

Step 6: Assume a passive attitude. . . .

Step 7: Continue for ten to twenty minutes.

Step 8: Practice the technique once or twice
daily.[14]

Not everyone will go into a hypnotic state through
Benson's Relaxation Response, but some surely will.

Self-Help Tapes

Ads for self-help tapes abound. Some of them promise the listener that if he listens to these tapes he will
be able to stop smoking, or lose weight, or gain self-
mastery. Such tapes guide the listener through certain
relaxation exercises and into a receptive state of mind
to receive soothing suggestions. The idea is that these
suggestions will bypass the conscious mind and reach
a subconscious or unconscious mind. Here again the
idea is that the real motivating power resides below
the surface of consciousness. And here again is another
opportunity to empty the mind and open it up to
demonic influence.

Unidentified Unexpected Places

In today's landscape of promises for self-fulfillment,
self-mastery, personal well-being, and quick fixes for

problems of living, one could easily find oneself in an environment conducive to hypnosis. You may recognize some of the inductive techniques being used innocently or purposefully and therefore be forewarned.

12

Conclusion

This book lists only some activities which call into question the use of hypnosis for Christians. There is a whole host of other phenomena which may occur during hypnosis. Everything from amnesia to automatic writing and from catalepsy (seizures) to crystal gazing are possibilities which await the hypnosis enthusiast.

Hypnosis is not simply a neutral, benign activity. Case reports have described individuals who have exhibited psychopathological symptoms following hypnosis and long-term negative effects.[1] As reported earlier, about ten percent of hypnotized individuals may suffer some difficulties related to their hypnotic experience. These occur in spite of the professional expertise or care that might be exercised. The risk is greater in group hypnosis.[2] Furthermore, long-term research regarding the results of hypnosis is scarce. Therefore negative effects could occur years later without anyone realizing the connection between negative effects and earlier hypnosis. Moreover, long-term spiritual effects of hypnosis on those who have submitted themselves to hypnotism have not been examined.

Hypnotism is potentially dangerous at its best and is demonic at its worst. At its worst hypnotism opens an individual to psychic experiences and satanic possession. When mediums go into hypnotic trances and contact the "dead," when clairvoyants reveal information which they could not possibly know, when fortunetellers through self-hypnosis reveal the future, Satan is at work. Hypnosis is an altered state of consciousness, and there is no difference between the altered state of consciousness and the shamanic state of consciousness.

Satan transforms himself into an angel of light whenever necessary to accomplish his schemes. If he can make an occult practice (hypnosis) look beneficial through a false facade (medicine or science), he will. It is obvious that hypnosis is lethal if used for evil purposes. However, we contend that hypnosis is potentially lethal for whatever purposes it is used. The moment one surrenders himself to the doorway of the occult, even in the halls of science and medicine, he is vulnerable to the powers of darkness.

An occult practice in the hands of even a kind-hearted doctor can still leave the Christian open to the works of the devil. Why would occultic hypnosis leave a person open to demonism and medical hypnosis not? Does the doctor have spiritual authority to keep Satan away? Is Satan afraid to interfere with science or medicine? When is the Ouija board merely a parlor game? Where is the boundary between a parlor game and the occult? When is hypnosis merely a medical or psychological tool? Where is the boundary between the medical or psychological and the occult? When does hypnosis move from the occult to medicine and from medicine to the occult? Why is it that some in the church who know that hypnosis has been an integral part of the occult nevertheless recommend its use? Paradoxically and sadly, though the experts cannot agree on what it is and how it works, hypnosis is being cultivated for Christian consumption.

Before hypnotism becomes the new panacea from the pulpit, followed by a plethora of books on the subject, its claims, methods, and long-term results should be considered. Arthur Shapiro has said, "One man's religion is another man's superstition and one man's magic is another man's science."[3] Hypnosis has become "scientific" and "medical" for some Christians with little proof of its validity, longevity of its results, or understanding of its nature. Because there are so many unanswered questions about its usefulness and so many potential dangers about its usage, Christians should shun hypnosis.

ENDNOTES

Chapter One: Hypnotic Origins
1. E. Fuller Torrey. *The Mind Game*. New York: Emerson Hall Publishers, Inc., 1972, p. 69.
2. *Self Hypnosis Tapes* Retail Catalogue. Grand Rapids: Potentials Unlimited, Inc., April 1982.
3. Walter Martin. "Hypnotism: Medical or Occultic." San Juan Capistrano: Christian Research Institute, audio cassette #C-74.
4. Josh McDowell and Don Stewart. *Understanding the Occult*. San Bernardino: Here's Life Publishers, Inc., 1982, p. 87.
5. Donald Gent letter, 11/20/87, p. 2.
6. H. Newton Maloney. *A Theology of Hypnosis*.
7. *The Christian Medical Society Journal*, Vol. XV, No. 2, Summer, 1984.
8. E. Thomas Dowd. "Hypnosis." *Psychotherapy Book News*, vol. 34, June 29, 2000, p. 18.
9. Robert C. Fuller. *Mesmerism and the American Cure of Souls*. Philadelphia: University of Pennsylvania Press, 1982, p. 1.
10. Jan Ehrenwalk, ed. *The History of Psychotherapy*. New Jersey: Jason Aronson Inc., 1991, p. 221.
11. Erika Fromm and Ronald Shor, eds. *Hypnosis: Development in Research and New Perspectives*. New York; Aldine Publishing Co., 1979, p. 20.
12. *Ibid.*, p. 10.
13. Fuller, *op. cit.*, p. 20.
14. *Ibid.*, pp. 46-47.
15. *Ibid.*, p. 104.
16. *Ibid.*, p. 45.
17. *Ibid.*
18. *Ibid.*, p. 46.
19. Robert C. Fuller. *Americans and the Unconscious*. New York: Oxford University Press, 1986, p. 36.
20. Fuller, *Mesmerism and the American Cure of Souls, op. cit.*, p. 152.
21. *Ibid.*, 12.
22. Thomas Szasz. *The Myth of Psychotherapy*. Garden City: doubleday/Anchor Press, 1978, p. 43.

Chapter Two: What Is Hypnosis?
1. "Hypnosis." *The Harvard Mental Health Letter*, Vol. 7, No. 10, April 1991, p. 1.
2. William Kroger and William Fezler. *Hypnosis and Behavior Modification: Imagery Conditioning*. Philadelphia: J. B. Lippincott Co., 1976, p. 14.
3. William Kroger. "No Matter How You Slice It, It's Hypnosis" audio. Garden Grove, CA: Infomedix.
4. Robert Baker. *They Call It Hypnosis*. Buffalo: Prometheus Books, 1990, p. 15.
5. *Ibid.*, p. 17.

6. Harold I. Kaplan and Benjamin J. Sadock. *Concise Textbook of Clinical Psychiatry*. Baltimore; Williams & Wilkins, 1996, p. 386.
7. *Ibid.*, p. 396.
8. Baker, *op. cit.*, p. 167.
9. Richard L. Gregory, ed. *The Oxford Companion to the Mind*. Oxford: Oxford University Press, 1987, p. 197.
10. Stephen M Kosslun et al. "Hypnotic Visual Illusion Alters Color Processing in the Brain," *American Journal of Psychiatry*, 157:8, August, 2000, p. 1279.
11. *Ibid.*, p. 1284.
12. David Spiegel. "Hypnosis," *The Harvard Mental Health Letter*, September, 1998, p. 5.
13. B. Bower. "Post-traumatic stress disorder: Hypnosis and the divided self." *Science News*, Vol. 133, No. 13, March 26, 1988, p. 197.
14. Erika Fromm quoted in *The Dallas Morning News*, April 13, 1987, p. D-9.
15. Joseph Barber. *Hypnosis and Suggestion in the Treatment of Pain*. New York: W.W. Norton & Company, 1996.p. 5.
16. Kaplan and Sadock, *op. cit.*, p. 396.
17. Raymond J. Corsini and Alan J. Auerbach. *Concise Encyclopedia of Psychology*. New York: John Wiley & Sons, Inc., 1998, p. 407.
18. Stephen G. Gilligan. *Therapeutic Trances: Cooperative Principles in Ericksonian Psychotherapy*. New York: Brunner/Mazel, 1987, pp. 46-59.
19. Michael Harner. *The Way of the Shaman*. San Francisco: Harper & Row, Publishers, 1980, p. 20.
20. *Ibid.*
21. Kenneth Ring. *Heading Toward Omega: In Search of the Meaning of the Near-Death Experience*. New York: William Morrow and Co., 1984.
22. Stanislov Grof. Book Review of *Heading Toward Omega* in *The Journal of Transpersonal Psychology*, Vol. 16, No. 2, pp. 245, 246.
23. Stanislov Grof from Angels, Aliens and Archetypes Symposium audiotape, San Francisco, November 1987. Mill Valley: Sound Photosynthesis.
24. Kaplan and Sadock, *op. cit.*, p. 242.
25. Corsini and Auerbach, *op. cit.*, p. 405.
26. Ernest Hilgard quoted by Donald Frederick, *op. cit.*, p. 5.
27. Carin Rubenstein, "Fantasy Addicts." *Psychology Today*, January 1981, p. 81.
28. Daniel Kohen, *Prevention*, July, 1985, p. 122.
29. Jeanne Achterberg. "Imagery in Healing: Shamanic and Modern Medicine," Mind & Supermind lecture, Santa Barbara, California, February 9, 1987.
30. William Kroger. "Healing with the Five Senses, " audio M253-8. Garden Grove, CA: InfoMedix.
31. Josephine Hilgard quoted by Corsini and Auerbach, *op. cit.*, p. 408.
32. Robert Baker. *They Call It Hypnosis*. Buffalo: Prometheus Books, 1990, p. 19.
33. *Ibid.*

34. Dave Hunt. *Occult Invasion*. Eugene, OR: harvest House Publishers, 1998, pp. 180-182.
35. Alan Morrison. *The Serpent and the Cross: Religious Corruption in an Evil Age*. Birmingham, UK: K & M Books, 1994, p. 426.
36. *Ibid.*, pp. 426, 427.
37. *Ibid.*, p. 432.

Chapter 3: Is Hypnosis a Natural Experience?

1. "Hypnosis in the Life of the Church," brochure for conference sponsored by Cedar Hill Institute for Graduate Studies, Twentynine Palms, CA, 1979, p. 1.
2. Ernest Hilgard quoted in *ibid.*
3. David Gordon, "The Fabric of Reality: Neurolinguistic Programming in Hypnosis." Talk sponsored by Santa Barbara City College, Santa Barbara, CA, January 19, 1981.
4. William Kroger and William Fezler. *Hypnosis and Behavior Modification: Imagery Conditioning*. Philadelphia: J. B. Lippincott Co., 1976, p. 19.
5. William Kroger. *Clinical and Experimental Hypnosis,* 2nd Ed. Philadelphia: J. B. Lippincott Co., 1977, p. 125.
6. Margaretta Bowers, "Friend or Traitor? Hypnosis in the Service of Religion." *International Journal of Clinical and Experimental Hypnosis,* 7:205, 1959.
7. Richard Morton. *Hypnosis and Pastoral Counseling*. Los Angeles: Westwood Publishing Co., 1980, p. 8.
8. *Ibid.*, p. 52.
9. *Ibid.*, p. 78.
10. *Ibid.*, pp. 78-79.
11. *Ibid.*, p. 84.

Chapter 4: Can the Will Be Violated?

1. Harold I. Kaplan and Benjamin J. Sadock. *Concise Textbook of Clinical Psychiatry*. Baltimore; Williams & Wilkins, 1996, p. 396.
2. Arthur Deikman. "Experimental Meditation." *Altered States of Consciousness*. Charles Tart, ed. Garden City: Anchor Books, 1972, p. 219.
3. Bernard Berelson and Gary Steiner. *Human Behavior*. New York: Harcourt, Brace & World, Inc., 1964 ,p. 125.
4. James J. Mapes. "Hypnosis: Stepping Beyond Entertainment." *Student Activities Programming*.
5. David Spiegel, "Hypnosis: New Research for Self Control." Mind and Supermind lecture series, Santa Barbara City College, January 20, 1987.
6. Ernest Hilgard, "Divided Consciousness in Hypnosis: The Implications of the Hidden Observer." *Hypnosis: Developments in Research and New Perspectives*. Erika Fromm and Ronald Shor, eds. New York: Aldine Publishing Company, 1979, p. 49.
7. Margaretta Bowers, "Friend or Traitor? Hypnosis in the Service of Religion." *International Journal of Clinical and Experi*mental *Hypnosis,* 7:205, 1959, p. 208.

8. Ernest Hilgard, "The Hypnotic State." *Consciousness: Brain, States of Awareness, and Mysticism, op. cit.*, p. 147.
9. Alfred Freedman, Harold Kaplan, and Benjamin Sadock. *Modern Synopsis of Comprehensive Textbook of Psychiatry / II.* Baltimore: The Williams and Wilkins Co., 1976, p. 905.
10. Simeon Edmonds. *Hypnotism and Psychic Phenomena,* North Hollywood: Wilshire Book Co., 1977, p. 141.
11. *Ibid.,* p. 139.
12. Martin Orne and Frederick Evans, "Social Control in the Psychological Experiment: Antisocial Behavior and Hypnosis." *Journal of Personality and Social Psychology,* Vol. 1, No. 3, p. 199.
13. Robert Blair Kaiser. *R.F.K. Must Die! A History of the Robert Kennedy Assassination and Its Aftermath.* New York: E.P. Dutton & Co, 1970, pp. 288-289.

Chapter 5: Induction/Seduction
1. Pierre Janet. *Psychological Healing: A Historical and Clinical Study,* trans. by Eden and Cedar Paul, Vol. 11. New York: Macmillan, 1925, p. 338.
2. William Kroger and William Fezler. *Hypnosis and Behavior Modification: Imagery Conditioning.* Philadelphia: J. B. Lippincott Co., 1976, pp. 25-26.
3. Keith Harary in *Psychology Today*, March-April, 1992, p. 59.
4. Marlene E. Hunter. *Creative Scripts for Hypnotherapy.* New York: Brunner/Mazel, Publishers, 1994, p. 3.
5. *Ibid.*, p. 5.
6. *Ibid.*
7. *Ibid.*, p. 6.
8. *Ibid.*
9. *Ibid.*, p. 10.
10. *Ibid.*, p. 11.
11. *Ibid.*, p. 11.
12. *Ibid.*, p. 11.
13. *Ibid.*
14. Harold I. Kaplan and Benjamin J. Sadock. *Concise Textbook of Clinical Psychiatry.* Baltimore; Williams & Wilkins, 1996, p. 396.
15. Kroger and Fezler, *op. cit.*, p. 17.
16. *Ibid.,* p. 30.
17. Daniel Goleman, "Secrets of a Modern Mesmer." Psychology Today, July 1977, pp. 62, 65.
18. Peter Francuch. Principles of Spiritual Hypnosis. Santa Barbara: Spiritual Advisory Press, 1981, p. 99.
19. Kroger and Fezler, *op. cit.*, p. 15.
20. Janet, *op. cit.*, p. 340.
21. Ernest Hilgard, "Divided Consciousness in Hypnosis: The Implications of the Hidden Observer." *Hypnosis: Developments in Research and New Perspectives.* Erika Fromm and Ronald Shor, eds. New York: Aldine Publishing Co., 1979, p. 55.
22. *Ibid.*, p. 49.
23. Janet, *op. cit.*, p. 338.

24. Thomas Szasz. *The Myth of Psychotherapy*. Garden City: Anchor Press/ Doubleday, 1978, p. 94.
25. E. Fuller Torrey. *The Mind Game*. New York: Emerson Hall Publishers Inc., 1972, p. 107.
26. *Ibid., p.* 107.
27. William Kroger. *Clinical and Experimental Hypnosis*, 2nd Ed. Philadelphia: J. B. Lippincott Co., 1977, p. 135.
28. Janet, *op. cit.,* p. 338.
29. Kroger and Fezler, *op. cit.,* p. xiii.
30. Kroger, *op. cit.,* p. 138.
31. *Ibid.,* p. 139.
32. "Expectations of Relief Alter Acupuncture Result." *Brain / Mind*, April 21, 1980. p. 1.
33. "False Feedback Eases Symptoms." *Brain / Mind*, June 16, 1980, pp. 1-2.
34. "Is There an Alpha Experience?" *Brain / Mind*, September 15, 1980, p. 2.
35. Christopher Cory, "Cooling By Deception." *Psychology Today*, June 1980, p. 20.
36. Arthur Shapiro interview. *The Psychological Society* by Martin Gross. New York: Random House, 1978, p. 230.
37. John S. Gillis, "The Therapist as Manipulator," *Psychology Today*, December 1974, p. 91.
38. *Ibid.,* p. 92.

Chapter 6: Age Regression and Progression

1. Mark Twain quoted in *FMS Foundation Newsletter*, August-September 1993, p. 2.
2. Michael D. Yapko. *Suggestions of Abuse: True and False Memories of Childhood Sexual Trauma*. New York: Simon & Schuster, 1994, p. 56.
3. John H. Edgette and Janet Sasson Edgette. *The Handbook of Hypnotic Phenomena in Psychotherapy*. New York: Brunner/Mazel Publishers, 1995, p. 104.
4. Raymond J. Corsini and Alan J. Auerbach. *Concise Encyclopedia of Psychology*. New York: John Wiley & Sons, Inc., 1998, p. 408.
5. *Brain / Mind*, February 15, 1982, p. 1.
6. *Ibid.,* pp. 1-2.
7. "Hypnotized Children Recall Birth Experiences." *Brain / Mind*, January 26, 1981, p. 1.
8. David Chamberlain quoted by Beth Ann Krier, "Psychologist Traces Problems Back to Birth." *Los Angeles Times,* February 26, 1981, Part V, p. 1.
9. Peter Francuch. *Principles of Spiritual Hypnosis*. Santa Barbara: Spiritual Advisory Press, 1981, p. 70. Used by permission.
10. Krier, *op. cit.,* p. 8.
11. Helen Wambach. *Reliving Past Lives: The Evidence Under Hypnosis*. New York: Harper and Row, 1978, cover.
12. Morris Netherton and Nancy Shiffrin. *Past Lives Therapy*. New York: William Morrow and Co., 1978.

13. *Ibid.*, pp. 114-122.
14. Gurny Williams III. "Mind, Body, Spirit." *Longevity*, December 1992, p. 68.
15. Dee Whittington, "Life After Death." *Weekly World News,* November 2, 1982, p. 17.
16. Paul Bannister, "1 in 5 Americans Has Lived Before on Other Planets." *National Enquirer,* March 9, 1982, p. 4.
17. Netherton and Shiffrin, *op. cit.,* back cover.
18. Kieron Saunders, "Hypnotic Predictions." *The Star,* July 22, 1980, p. 11.
19. William Kroger. *Clinical and Experimental Hypnosis.* 2nd Ed. Philadelphia: J. B. Lippincott Co., 1977, p. 18.
20. "Future Lives." *Omni,* October 1987, p. 128.
21. Edgette and Edgette, *op. cit.,* p. 127.
22. *Ibid.*, pp. 127-128.
23. "The Power of Mental Persuasion." *Longevity*, May 1991, p. 97.
24. Francuch, *op. cit.,* p. 70.
25. *Ibid.,* p. 24.

Chapter 7: Hypnotic Memory

1. Ernest Hilgard. *Divided Consciousness: Multiple Controls in Human Thought and Action.* New York: John Wiley and Son, 1977, p. 43.
2. Carol Tavris, "The Freedom to Change." *Prime Time,* October 1980, p. 28.
3. *Harvard Mental Health Letter*, February 1998, p. 5.
4. Glenn S. Sanders and William L. Simmons, "Use of Hypnosis to Enhance Eyewitness Accuracy: Does It Work?" *Journal of Applied Psychology*, Vol. 68, No. 1, 1983, p. 70.
5. Robert Baker. *They Call It Hypnosis.* Buffalo: Prometheus Books, 1990, p. 194.
6. *Ibid.*
7. Elizabeth Loftus quoted in *ibid*, p. 195.
8. *JAMA* 1985, Vol. 253, p. 1918.
9. *Ibid.*, p. 1920.
10. Robert A. Baker. *Hidden Memories.* Buffalo: Prometheus Books, 1992, p. 152.
11. *Ibid.*, p. 154.
12. *Ibid.*, p. 155.
13. "Reaching Back for a 'Past Life." *Orlando Sentinel*, November 2, 1991, p. E-1.
14. Michael Ypako quoted in *FMS Foundation Newsletter*, August-September, 1993, p. 3.
15. "Recovered Memories: Are They Reliable?" False Memory Syndrome Foundation, 1955 Locust Street, Philadelphia, PA 19103-5766.
16. *Calgary Herald*, Nov. 16, 1998, quoted in *FMS Foundation Newsletter*, Vol. 8, No. 1, 1999.
17. Bernard L. Diamond, "Inherent Problems in the Use of Pretrial Hypnosis on a Prospective Witness." *California Law Review,* March 1980, p. 348.
18. *Ibid.,* p. 314.

19. "State Supreme Court Rejects Hypnosis Testimony." *Santa Barbara News-Press,* March 12, 1982, p. A-16.
20. Beth Ann Krier, "When the Memory Plays Tricks." *Los Angeles Times,* December 4, 1980, Part V, p. 1.
21. Susan Riepe, "Remembrance of Times Lost." *Psychology Today,* November 1980, p. 99.
22. Diamond, *op. cit.,* pp. 333-337. Used by permission.

Chapter 8: Deep Hypnosis

1. Charles Tart, "Measuring Hypnotic Depth." *Hypnosis: Developments in Research and New Perspectives.* Erika Fromm and Ronald Shor, eds. New York: Aldine Publishing Company, 1979, p. 590.
2. *Ibid.,* p. 593.
3. *Ibid.,* p. 594.
4. *Ibid.,* p. 596.
5. Daniel Goleman and Richard Davidson. *Consciousness: Brain, States of Awareness, and Mysticism.* New York: Harper and Row, 1979, p. 46.
6. Harold I. Kaplan and Benjamin J. Sadock. *Concise Textbook of Clinical Psychiatry.* Baltimore; Williams & Wilkins, 1996, p. 242.
7. Melvin Gravitz quoted by Frederick, "Hypnosis Awaking from a Deep Sleep." *Los Angeles Times,* December 10, 1980, Part I-A, p. 5.
8. Erika Fromm, "Altered States of Consciousness and Hypnosis: A Discussion." *The International Journal of Clinical and Experimental Hypnosis,* October 1977, p. 326.
9. Jeanne Achterberg. "Imagery in Healing: Shamanic and Modern Medicine." Mind and Supermind lecture series, Santa Barbara City College, February 9, 1987.
10. Michael Harner. *The Way of the Shaman.* San Francisco: Harper & Row, Publishers, 1980, p. 49.
11. *Ibid.,* pp. 49-50.
12. *Ibid.,* p. 136.
13. Ernest Hilgard. *Divided Consciousness: Multiple Controls in Human Thought and Action.* New York: John Wiley and Sons, 1977, p. 168.
14. Peter Francuch. *Principles of Spiritual Hypnosis.* Santa Barbara: Spiritual Advisory Press, 1981, p. 79. Used by permission.
15. *Ibid.,* p. 80.
16. Ernest R. Hilgard, Rita L. Atkinson, and Richard C. Atkinson. *Introduction to Psychology,* 7th Ed. New York: Harcourt Brace Jovanovich, Inc., 1979, p. 179.
17. David Haddon, "Meditation and the Mind." *Spiritual Counterfeits Project Newsletter,* January 1982, p. 2.
18. *Ibid.,* p. 2.
19. William Kroger. *Clinical and Experimental Hypnosis,* 2nd Ed. Philadelphia: J. B. Lippincott Co., 1977, p. 126.
20. Ernest Hilgard, *Divided Consciousness, op. cit.,* p. 20.
21. "Hypnosis in Court," KNX, Los Angeles, Newsradio editorial reply, April 7, 1982.
22. Peter Francuch. *Messages from Within.* Santa Barbara: Spiritual Advisory Press, 1982, publicity flyer.

Chapter 9: Hypnosis: Medical, Scientific, or Occultic?

1. Donald Hebb, "Psychology Today/The State of the Science." *Psychology Today,* May 1982, p. 53.
2. Thomas Szasz. *The Myth of Psychotherapy.* Garden City: Anchor Press/ Doubleday, 1978, pp. 185-186.
3. E. Fuller Torrey. *The Mind Game.* New York: Emerson Hall Publishers, Inc., 1972, p. 70.
4. William Kroger. *Clinical and Experimental Hypnosis,* 2nd Ed. Philadelphia: J. B. Lippincott Co., 1977, p. 122.
5. *Ibid.,* p. 123.
6. William Kroger and William Fezler. *Hypnosis and Behavior Modification: Imagery Conditioning.* Philadelphia: J. B. Lippincott Co., 1976, p. 412.
7. Helen Benson, "Hypnosis Seen as Tool to Bond Body, Mind." *Santa Barbara News-Press,* May 31, 1982, p. B-1.
8. "A Special Talent for Self-Regulation." *Human Potential,* December, 1985, p. 15.
9. Bobgan letter, September 11, 1985, on file.
10. Ernest Hilgard letter, September 15, 1985, on file.
11. *Ibid.*
12. Joseph Palotta. *The Robot Psychiatrist.* Metairie, LA: Revelation House Publishers, Inc., 1981, p. 11.
13. *Ibid.,* p. 177.
14. *Ibid.,* p.400.
15. Szasz, *op. cit.,* p. 133.
16. Joseph Palotta. "Medical Hypnosis: Pulling Down Satan's Strongholds." *Christian Medical Society Journal,* Vol. XV, No. 2, summer 1984, p. 9.
17. *Ibid.*
18. "The Master Course in Advanced Hypnotherapy" advertisement, Hypnotism Training Institute of Los Angeles.
19. Potentials Unlimited Self-Hypnosis Tapes catalog, Grand Rapids, Michigan.
20. Szasz, *op. cit.,* p. 185.
21. "Sophrology: Neutralizing Stress, Enhancing Physical Performance." *Brain / Mind,* October 26, 1981, pp. 1-2.
22. John Weldon and Zola Levitt. *Psychic Healing.* Chicago: Moody Press, 1982, p. 32.
23. *Ibid.,* p. 7.
24. Arthur Deikman. *The Observing Self – Mysticism and Psychotherapy.* Los Altos: ISHK Book Service, advertising flyer.
25. *TM In Court.* Berkeley: Spiritual Counterfeits Project, 1978.
26. Ralph Metzner. *Maps of Consciousness.* New York: Macmillan Co., 1971.
27. David Gelman et al. "Illusions that Heal." *Newsweek,* November 17, 1986, p. 74.
28. *The Dallas Morning News,* April 13, 1987, p. 9D.
29. Ernest R. Hilgard quoted in "Illusions that Heal," *op. cit.,* p. 75.
30. Hilgard and Hilgard (1986) quoted by Robert A. Baker. "Hypnosis and Pain Control," *New Realities,* March/April 1991, p. 28.

31. Nathan Szajnberg and Seymour Diamond. "Biofeedback, Migraine Headache and New Symptom Formation." *Headache Journal*, 20:29-31.
32. Weldon and Levitt, *op. cit.,* p. 195.
33. Kurt Koch. *Demonology: Past and Present.* Grand Rapids: Kregel Publications, 1973, p. 121.
34. Weldon and Levitt, *op. cit., p.* 110.
35. Kurt Koch. *Occult Bondage and Deliverance.* Grand Rapids: Kregel Publications, 1970, p. 40.
36. Kurt Koch. *Occult ABC.* Trans. by Michael Freeman. Germany: Literature Mission Aglasterhausen, Inc., 1978, p. 98.
37. Alfred Freedman et al. *Modern Synopsis of Comprehensive Textbook of Psychiatry/II,* 2 ed. Baltimore: The Williams & Wilkins Co., 1976, p. 905.

Chapter 10: The Bible and Hypnosis

1. Dr. Maurice M. Tinterow. *Foundations of Hypnosis from Mesmer to Freud.* Springfield: Charles C. Thomas Publisher, 1970, p. x.
2. Dave Hunt. *The Cult Explosion.* Eugene: Harvest House Publishers, 1980.
3. Dave Hunt. *Occult Invasion.* Eugene: Harvest House Publishers, 1998.
4. Dave Hunt, personal letter to Walter Martin, January 13, 1982, p. 5.
5. "Hypnosis." *Profiles.* Arlington, TX: Watchman Fellowhip, 1998.
6. John Weldon and Zola Levitt. *Psychic Healing.* Chicago: Moody Press, 1982, p. 10.
7. "Hypnosis may be hazardous." *Psychology Today*, June 1987, p. 21.
8. Richard Watring. "New Age Training in Business." *Eternity*, February 1988, p. 31.
9. Paul C. Reisser. "Holistic Health Update." *Spiritual Counterfeits Project Newsletter*, September-October 1983, p. 3.
10. Donald Vittner letter, August 11, 1980, on file.
11. Robert M. Johnson. *A Logic Book*, 2nd Ed. Belmont, CA: Wadsworth Publishing company, 1992, p. 258.
12. H. Newton Maloney. "A Theology for Hypnosis," unpublished position paper.
13. George Newbold. "Hypnotherapy and Christian Belief." *Christian Medical Society Journal*, Vol. XV, No. 2., Summer 1984, p. 7.
14. *Ibid.*, p. 6.

Chapter 11: Hypnosis in Unexpected Places

1. Michael Ypako quoted in *FMS Foundation Newsletter*, August-September, 1993, p. 3.
2. Campbell Perry. *Hypnos*, Vol. XXII, No. 4, p. 189.
3. Mark Pendergrast. *Victims of Memory: Incest Accusations and Shattered Lives.* Hinesburg, VT: Upper Access, Inc., 1995, p. 129.
4. Agnes Sanford. *The Healing Gifts of the Spirit.* Philadelphia: J.B. Lippincot, 1966, p. 125.
5. Jane Gumprecht. *Abusing Memory: The Healing Theology of Agnes Sanford.* Moscow, ID: Canon Press, 1997, pp. 104-105.
6. *Ibid.*, p. 106.

7. Michael Yapko quoted by Ave Opincar. "Speak, Memory." *San Diego Weekly Reader*, August 19, 1993.
8. Michael Harner. *The Way of the Shaman*. New York: Harper & Row, Publishers, 1980m p. 31.
9. David Tame. *The Secret Power of Music*. Rochester, VT: Destiny Books, 1984, p. 170.
10. *Ibid.*, p. 176.
11. "Hypnosis in the Life of the Church," brochure for conference sponsored by Cedar Hill Institute for Graduate Studies, Twentynine Palms, CA, 1979, p. 1.
12. Walter W. Surwillow and Douglas P. Hobson. "Brain Electrical Activity During Prayer." *Psychological Reports*, Vol. 43, 1978, p. 140.
13. Herbert Benson with William Proctor. "Your Maximum Mind," *New Age Journal*, November/December 1987, p. 19.
14. *Ibid.*

Chapter 12: Conclusion

1. Moris Kleinhauz and Barbara Beran. "Misuse of Hypnosis: A Factor in Psychopathology," *American Journal of Clinical Hypnosis*, Vol. 26, No. 3, January 1984, pp. 283-290.
2. Pamela Knight. "Hypnosis may be hazardous." *Psychology Today*, January 1987, p. 20.
3. Arthur Shapiro, "Hypnosis, Miraculous Healing, and Ostensibly Supernatural Phenomena." *A Scientific Report on the Search for Bridey Murphy*. M. Kline, ed. New York: Julian Press, 1956, p. 147.

For a sample copy of a free newsletter about the intrusion of psychological counseling theories and therapies into the church, please write to:

PsychoHeresy Awareness Ministries
4137 Primavera Road
Santa Barbara, CA 93110

<http://www.psychoheresy-aware.org>

Books by Martin & Deidre Bobgan

PSYCHOHERESY: The Psychological Seduction of Christianity exposes fallacies and failures of psychological counseling theories and therapies. Reveals anti-Christian biases, internal contradictions, and documented failures of secular psychotherapy; and examines amalgamations with Christianity and explodes firmly entrenched myths that undergird these unholy unions. 272 pages, softbound.

COMPETENT TO MINISTER: The Biblical Care of Souls calls Christians back to the Bible and mutual care in the Body of Christ, encourages personal ministry among Christians, and equips believers to minister God's grace through biblical conversation, prayer, and practical help. 252 pages, softbound.

THE END OF "CHRISTIAN PSYCHOLOGY" reveals that "Christian psychology" includes contradictory theories and techniques; describes and analyzes major psychological theories influencing Christians; shows that professional psychotherapy with its underlying psychologies is questionable at best, detrimental at worst, and a spiritual counterfeit at least; and challenges the church to rid itself of all signs and symptoms of this scourge. 290 pages, softbound.

FOUR TEMPERAMENTS, ASTROLOGY & PERSONALITY TESTING examines personality types and tests from a biblical, historical, and research basis. 214 pages, soft-bound.

More books by Martin & Deidre Bobgan

JAMES DOBSON'S GOSPEL OF SELF-ESTEEM & PSYCHOLOGY demonstrates that many of Dobson's teachings are based on godless, secular opinions. Self-esteem and psychology are the two major thrusts of his ministry that supersede sin, salvation, and sanctification. They are another gospel. 248 pages, softbound.

LARRY CRABB'S GOSPEL traces Crabb's 22-year journey of jolts, shifts, and expansions as he has sought to create the best combination of psychology and the Bible. Crabb's eclectic theories and methods remain psychologically bound and consistent with current psychotherapy trends. This book provides a detailed analysis. 210 pages, softbound.

12 STEPS TO DESTRUCTION: Codependency/Recovery Heresies examines codependency/recovery teachings, Alcoholics Anonymous, twelve-step groups, and addiction treatment programs from a biblical, historical, and research perspective and urges believers to trust in the sufficiency of Christ and the Word of God. 256 pages, softbound.

THEOPHOSTIC COUNSELING ~ Divine Revelation? or PsychoHeresy? examines a recovered memory therapy comprised of many existent psychological therapies and techniques, demon deliverance teachings, and elements from the inner healing movement, which include guided imagery, visualization, and hypnosis. 144 pages, soft-bound.

MISSIONS & PSYCHOHERESY exposes the mental health profession's false façade of expertise for screening missionary candidates and caring for missionaries. It explodes myths about psychological testing and reveals the prolific practice of using mental health professionals to provide care for missionaries suffering from problems of living. 168 pages, softbound.

AGAINST "BIBLICAL COUNSELING": FOR THE BIBLE reveals what biblical counseling is, rather than what it pretends or hopes to be. Its primary thrust is to call Christians back to the Bible and to biblically ordained ministries and mutual care in the Body of Christ. 200 pages, softbound.

CRI GUILTY OF PSYCHOHERESY? answers the CRI-Passantino "Psychology & the Church" series, exposes their illogical reasoning, and argues that supporting psychotherapy and its underlying psychologies is an opprobrium in the church. 152 pages, softbound.